AF540830

Migrant Labour in India

MIGRANT LABOUR IN INDIA

S. N. TRIPATHY
&
C. R. DASH

Discovery Publishing House
New Delhi—110 002

First Published—1997
Reprinted: 2013

ISBN 81–7141–384–6

Published by :

Discovery Publishing House
4831/24, Ansari Road, Prahlad Street
Darya Ganj, New Delhi—110 002 (INDIA)
Phone : 327 92 45
Fax.: 91-11-3253475

Laser Typeset by :

Allied Computers,
Karnal (Haryana)

Printed at :
Dynamic printers, Delhi

Contents

Preface

Man is constantly on move. Migration implies the phenomenon of the flow of people over shorter or longer destinations either for temporary or permanent settlement. Labour migration may be defined as a form of labour mobility towards districts or states or out-side where industry and employment are expanding. Infact, the history of population migration is as old as man itself.

The vital streams of labour migration are rural-rural, rural-urban and urban-rural. Since the principal current of modern migration all over the world is towards urban areas, the present work addresses itself to the problem of the rural-urban migration in Orissa.

Rural-urban migration reduces population pressure in rural areas, but economic problems remain unsolved as simply transferred to urban areas. The illiterate, less educated, unskilled landless, agricultural migrant labourers only aggravate the pressure on informal employment sector (Surat-Oriya migrants in the current analysis).

In the back drop of the aforesaid factors, the researchers investigated the causes underlying the process of migration.

In the absence of a detailed study, the present work is claimed to be the first such study ever attempted confining to Ganjam district of Orissa, where migration is of paramount significance to national development. The study focuses on the volume and direction of inter-state migrant workers like dadan out migrants, Surat migrants and all other types of labour migrants alongwith their demographic socio-economic features.

The analysis yield insights concerning population distribution and effects of migration on population growth. The analytical part has been based on data collected for the purpose through sample surveys. The study in general and regional analysis in particular, provides a necessary base for further research into the underlying reasons of migration and its socio-economic sequal.

In the preparation of this work, we have received immense help and encouragements from Prof. Prahallad Panda, Prof. Baidyanath Misra and others.

We also owe an immense debt to the respondent households and to the officials who cooperated with us in our enquiry.

We shall feel amply rewarded, if the work is of some help in comprehending the complex problems of migrant labourers and in improving the organisational machinery to tackle them.

Finally, the authors, of course, hold themselves responsible for any short-comings the study may suffer from.

S.N. Tripathy
C.R. Dash

1

History and Origin of Labour Migration

This chapter portrays the genesis of labour migration in Indian states with special reference to Orissa, besides this chapter also unfolds the overview of literature with a view of identifying research gaps, justifying the rationale of the study.

From literature and available records it has been ascertained with agricultural labourers existed in ancient and medieval India. But there is dearth of data with regard to numbers or magnitude of such labourers. But it is generally believed that the class of landless labourers was created during the British rule in India. During the said period, the flooding of India with foreign manufacturers, destroyed domestic industries, and so drove the artisan on to the land. The British introduced a system under which land revenue was assessed at high rates and was payable in cash which held individuals responsible for payment. However, economic historian Mr. Sukomal Sen has remarked, "In the construction of railways in India, first germinated the modern India working class.[1]

These landless poverty stricken labourers began to migrate to various colonies like British Guiana, West Indies, Mauritius as a result of abolition of slave trade and slave system in 1807 and 1834 respectively. There was acute shortage of labour in the British colonies and it was the Indian labourers who were sought to be introduced in the plantation of these colonies. Poverty-stricken Indian labourers were exported to such colonies. Thus, the emigrant Indian labour was another victim of brutal colonial exploitation.[2]

Throughout the 19th century the British India witnessed a formidably growing unemployment in the ranks of the landless poor masses with the steady decline of traditional economy alongwith rapid growth of population. It was these destitute masses who migrated from India to overseas British colonies as indentured labour. Available data indicate that during 1870 more than half a million labourers - men, women and children collected from various parts of India were thus, exported to British colonies.[3]

In the 1830s and 1840s, the recruiting ground was mainly the tribal areas. Most of the emigrants were so called "hill coolies" who were recruited from Chotanagpur division, Shahabad, Bankura, Birbhum and Bardhan districts of Bengal Presidency.[4]

The Plantation Labour

After 1840's the number going to the colonies gradually declined party because of heavy mortality at sea among the class of emigrants and partly due to the competition of the tea districts of Assam. It was reported that in South India, "the largest number is drawn from Godavary, Vizag, Ganjam district and from Madras and Chingleput.[5]

Whenever there was any scarcity or famine in Bengal presidency, the arkatis could recruit a sufficient number of labourers from Bengal presidency. Thus, in the seasons of 1867-68 and 1869, the greatest proportion of recruits were drawn from Bengal and chiefly from its south-western frontier—Cuttack, Midnapur, Bankura etc., where scarcity and famine occurred.[6]

The origin of debt among the landed classes was traceable to various causes, among which the most prominent were the failure of crops from droughts, expenditure on marriage or other ceremonies, general thribtlessness, and improvident use of sudden inflation of credit, unsuitable revenue settlements.[7]

An increase in the number of members of the family, a rise in rent, the growth of debt, all contribute to force the agricultural labourers to abandon his ancestral occupation.

Poverty, though a significant factor, is not the only disability which drives the villagers to the factory. Suffered from serious social disabilities the lower castes long for migration to individual centres. Their growing realisation of their humiliated position and the prospects of freedom in Industrial centres insists them to migrate to escape from the sufferings of social disabilities.[8]

The Royal commission on labour (1929–31) further observed that Orisan labourers used to go Rangoon, Assam, Bengal and Bombay since 1803 in order to work in plantations, earth work dams ,roads, railways, jute mills, textile mills etc. To eke out a living, the labourers of Orissa migrate to distant parts of the country being forced by natural calamities like famine and high pressure of population on land, absence of alternative avenues of employment etc. The exploitation by the feudal lords by the princely states of Orissa had worked as a push factor for such out migration.

Even various agricultural labour enquiry reports corroborates the above facts. It has been remarked that in the district of Cuttack, it was customary to employ gangs of ten or twenty labourers in the month of February, March and April. These gangs came from outside the district, mostly from Ganjam and were engaged for sinking wells or excavating tanks, land sepairs or reclamation of waste lands or sand beds. They were paid a preferential wage of Rs. 1–8 a day, the local rate being Rs. 1 to Rs. 1–4 for such operations.[9] The gangs consisted of males and laboured for six hours a day i.e. from 7 a.m. to 1 AM and 3 p.m. to 5 p.m.. They cooked their mid-day meal during the rest interval. It was reported that these labourers from outside were hard working and honest and did not require much supervision on the part of the employer.

A large segment of migrant labourers in Orissa belong to the category of landless agricultural labourers, and very often from scheduled, backward or tribal castes. In few cases those who have limited land didn't possess the needed resource to develop the same and as a result, the barred land is left uncultivated for years. Therefore, they are, compelled to work as agricultural labourers in the land of the big landlords or Zamindars of the same village or adjoining villages. The employment being seasonal and the wages being low, they find it hard to make both ends meet. Thus, the insufficiency of such labourers income to cover the living expenses even on a subsistence level seems to be the basic underlying factor of their indebtedness.[10] Further, the social customs and obligations like births, marriages, death in the families and drinking habits play an important role in forcing the poor to resort the borrowings. The money lenders use to take advantages of the deteriorating economic conditions of the poor. They advance small loans from time to time in exchange of binding them to work as agricultural labourers till the final payment is made. Thus, indebtedness has been generally believed to have emerged as a factor challenging the economic self-sufficiency of such labourers who find it difficult to repay. Their dues accumulate very fast under exorbitantly high rates of interest. They find it impossible to extinguish their debts and begin to work for the creditor at extremely low wages and venture to repay the debt by their hard labour. At this critical time, the Sardars or khatadars the recruiting agents of brick-kiln owners or stone quarry lessees or construction project contractors, approach such labourers. They make false promises and allure the poverty stricken labourers to the distant land.

As each labourer is paid a part of his due for the labour he would render before he goes to the work-site in advance and the rest after the period of contract is over the practice followed is well named after the Dadan labour. The agricultural labourers unable to understand the problems and agony involved at the time of receiving such advance from the recruiting agents or contractors.

Elements of Exploitation

The tragic fact is that no sooner they reach at the work site, than all the hopes disappear and promises made to them undermine. Moreover, they are subjected to a chain of merciless exploitation in the hands of munshis of the brick kiln owner or stone quarry lessees. They are made to work pretty long hours, not being provided with medical benefits, proper food and shelter. Illiterate and ignorant of any other language except Oriya, they fail to putforth their legitimate grievances before the local non-oriya authorities and therefore, the latters in all possible manner fail to come to the former's rescue. The Dadan labour of Orissa are taken to far off places like Jammu and Kashmir, Meghalaya, Sikkim and even to the Arabian countries like Iraq and Iran. The recruitment of Dadan labourers in Orissa is made mostly from the rural and tribal areas of Keonjhar, Mayurbhanja, Sambalpur, Bolangir, Kalahandi, Ganjam and Puri district.

Stricken Kalahandi —The Mishra Report

There are reliable report[11] with regard to mass migration of labourers to the neighbouring states due to long spell of drought in the poverty stricken tribal district of Kalahandi. In the district of Kalahandi during the year 1990 there accrued a large-scale migration in some villages like Udaypur, Dongriguda Chhatikuda and Jhikimiki villagers in large number have left their homes with women and children and their houses were collapsed due to their long absence.

There are repeated cases of sale of child, bonded labour, starvation death and frequent out break of diseases in Kalahandi.

Tribal Migrants of Orissa

During the British period, under the impact of new politico-administrative measures, the tribals of Orissa last their moorings from the tribal economy tribal social organisation, tribal religion and tribal cultural life. A large section of this population was reduced to the status of bond slaves or agrestic serfs of money lenders, Zamindars and contractors who emerged in Indian society as as equal of the political and economic policies pursued by the British. Another section was reduced to the category of near slave labourers or 'Dadan' labourers, labouring on plantations, in mines, railways and road construction and other projects.[12]

Prof. Saha also viewed similar conclusion in the state of Bihar tribals remarked, "There was another device by which the tribal people were forced to work as bond servant in the fields of money lenders. They would became Kamia or the bond servant of creditors. This Kamia system came into vogue with the immigrant speculators from Bihar. They succeeded like the eupatrids of early Athenian history...........in making bond slaves of concer classes by sheer power of money."[13]

The Present Scenario

In Bolangir, Kalahandi and Phulbani—the backward district of Orissa because of the deforestation increased pressure on land, lack of irrigation and recurring drought conditions due to poverty and unemployment, tribals have been migrating to outside villages districts and state for periods ranging from 2 to 6 months for working in construction projects bricks-kilns and tea estates.[14]

Exploitation of tribal and agricultural labourers are common phenomenon in Patnagarh and Titilagarh sub-division of Bolangir. Earlier it had been observed that the economic plight put them almost in the point of starvation leading to pledge their services to the gaontias.[15]

The Brick-kiln Migrant Labourers

It has been observed by the researchers that every year during march to June thousands of tribals from Bolangir and Kalahandi migrate out-side the state in search of employment. They are employed in brick industries located at Patrapur, Itchapuram, Palasa, Srikakulam in the neighbouring state of Andhra Pradesh. They toil hard from 6 AM morning to 10 PM night. There is no specific work-hour and as a result, the more they work, the more they earn. For each piece of brick, they get 20 paise only. Each brick kiln labourer builds at least 600 bricks each day, labouring for 12 to 13 hours. For preparation of clay, water and mixture for bricks they devote the morning hours and in the afternoon shifts they construct bricks such tribal labourers of Bolangir and Kalahandi are mostly unskilled. However, they are habituated with working in brick kiln industries. They move in group alongwith their wives and children who also put hard labour for their survival. They could not understand Hindi nor could not speak Oriya language properly. Some of them are also found in various brick-kilns of Berhampur, Purosottampur, Sheragada in Ganjam district of Orissa.

It is revealed that factors like famines, loss of land through indebtedness, acute unemployment in the place of origin, caste disabilities, destruction of village crafts are push factors of the tribal migrants of Bolangir and Kalahandi.

Medical facilities, weekly holidays, statutory leaves, bonus and other labour laws[16] are never observed in case of such tribal migrants of Bolangir and Kalahandi (Orissa).

Inhuman Exploitation

Such illiterate, less educated, unorganised tribal labourers of Bolangir and Kalahandi (Janagarh and Boden blocks) are exploited by the brick industry owners. They experience untold misery and horrible plight not only in he work-site but also inside the state transport bus. Inside the bus, they are not provided with tickets, in most cases nor even seats. Short route passengers bearing good dresses occupy seats but these poor, dirty clothed tribals were discriminated and even fail to catch the sympathy the bus conductors.

They work in the filthy working conditions, devoid of safety measures. They suffer from tuberculosis, asthma, respiratory infections and long-cancer but no medical assistance is available to them. The tribal migrants are docile, submissive and subservient to the employer.

Some agricultural labourers from Bolangir and Kalahandi are also found migrating to Raipur, Jagdalpur, Nagpur and Surath for working in various construction projects and to pull rickshaw.

The foregoing analysis brought to light that labour out-migration has been a continuous phenomenon in our country and more correctly among the poor segments of society. It should be kept in view that migration being the movement of human beings in pursuit of certain cherished objects like better employment, better wages and better quality of life, there is apparently nothing wrong. However, the problem is of serious magnitude when such migration into human misery and exploitation.

Research Gaps and Issues

To get a better insight into the problem of labour migration, a brief review of available studies on migration has been presented below. The review intends to identity research gaps on the topic which would help us to raise some issues for detailed discussion in the study.

Literature on migrant labour are available in Indian context, in recent years. As early as in 1929-31, the Royal Commission on labour highlighted the existence of migrant labour in Indian states.

A systematic attempt to examine the mobility of population in India through census statistics was made by Davis (1951)[17] He has studied the immobile nature of Indian population due to the factors like dominance of agriculture, caste system early marriage, joint family, language barriers and illiteracy.

Prabhu (1956)[18] attempted to study the social effects of urbanisation on Industrial labourers migrating from rural areas to the city of Bombay.

Sovani (1959)[19] has made a population study in which potential out-migrants in three districts of Orissa were taken as removable surplus population.

Jachariah (1964)[20] made a detailed investigation into internal migration in the Indian sub-continent during 1901-31 in order to measure and narrate its magnitude, assess its contribution to the process of population redistribution.

George (1966)[21] confined his study to two states West Bengal and Assam and dealt with the estimation of volume of migration at the district level in a historical perspective from 1901 to 1961.

Vaid (1968)[22] has studied the migrant status of the industrial labourers at Kota region.

An indispensable source is the report of the National commission on labour (1969)[23] which brings together a large amount of historical and statistical information and industrial and other labour, with a good critical discussion of issues like the relation between the "Organised" and "unorganised" sectors; political obstacles to labour migration between Indian states, choice of techniques and their social outcome etc.

Prof. Saha (1970)[24] has made a unique study bringing abut the historical factors underlying out-migration of Indian labourers to British Sugar Colonies—Guiana, Trinidad, Jumica and Mahritius, especially after the abolition of slavery in 1834. The form of the labour supply was indentured labour due to the demands of the Sugar colonies. This was due to the search by British capitalists for an ample supply of cheap and easily controlled labour. This labour supply was mainly from India as the latter was under British control. Emigration of Indian labour, began on an organised scale in 1834 and continued till 1917. In 1900–1901, nearly half a million labourers of Indian origin was living in those sugar colonies. This out-migration of hill coolies and tribal labourers of India was due to abject poverty and oppression by the Zamindars. They were rack rented by the tickadars, or Sardars. Because of feudal and social oppression which made them almost pauper, this emigration of the lower caste people was the sequel.

Srivastav and Ali (1981)[25] have analysed the behaviour of migrant labourers and remarked that oscillatory migrants do not abandon their place of origin. In Bundelkhand region, especially, the kols were facilitated by professional labour contractors. The contractors attract the kols advancing loans at the time of their social urgency and employ them in various work sites. Adults in age group of 15-35, females and even children were employed in such works like kendu leaves, plucking, construction works etc.

Kamble (1983)[26] examined the problem of labour migration in the state of Kerala on the basis of primary data and simple statistical tools. The study has been reported in eight chapters covering both in and out-migration, their volume, type, direction of movement educational levels, occupations etc. to find out who were out-migrating and who were in-migrating people.

Breman (1985)[27] conducted a study in the state of Gujarat especially, in Bardoli taluka, this study revealed the fact that the capitalistic form of farming has caused inequality in rural areas resulting in increasing polarisation of classes between the landowners and the landless labourers.

The migrant labour is exceedingly vulnerable to exploitation. The farmers requires them only for a limited part of the year to perform tasks which required little or no skill. They have to be satiated with distressed and long, irregular working hours, easy to employ at short notice and of the same time immediately replacable.

Singh (1986)[28] examined the characteristic patterns of rural to urban migration in three Indian states—Bihar, West Bengal and Kerala - basing upon census data, in a cross cultural perspective. The study points that different social, cultural and economic structures have a definite impact on the differentials in rural to Urban migration.

Nijam Khan (1986)[29] presents a picture of the persistence of depressed and stagnant agricultural economy that had hardly exhibited any sign of improvement. The study has been based on the field data collected from twenty randomly selected villages of Uttar Pradesh and explores the pattern of migration on the basis of quantum of migration, characteristics of migrants, spatio-temporal pattern of movement, and migrants contract with the community of origin. The study has brought to light that economic backwardness in rural areas caused by appalling lack of gainful employment opportunities and inability of meagre land to absorb the tremors of population explosion has been pushing rural bulk to greener pastures of urban centres in search of livelihood. Migration was initially seasonal in character as remarked by Najma Khan, but has lately become a permanent feature.

Vidut Joshi (1987)[30] focused the horrible plights of migrants workmen employed in Government projects in Uttar-Kashi, Uttar Pradesh (Tehri Garhwal Project). Labourers from Orissa, Bihar including women and children were employed in such project works violating all labour laws, like Inter state migrant workmen (Regulation of employment and conditions of service) Act, 1979. Most of such labourers especially from Orissa were dadan labourers who had received advance from the labour contractors.

Subrahmanya (1987)[31] in his article, 'Policy and Administrative aspects of labour migration', has remarked that migrant labourers were mainly seasonal character and generally, associated with the features of contract labour or bonded labour.

An ICSSR Project study[32] (1987) mainly examined the socio-economic conditions of dadan out-migrant labourers of Ganjam district (Orissa). Such out-migrants (dadan labourers) reportedly suffer exploitation and harassment at the hands of agents who recruit them and also the principal employers who provide them employment. Though a very old system, the dadan out-migration was potraged as an institution of exploitation by the press in early 70's with the help of survey method, the study had been conducted to collect information pertaining to the socio-economic conditions of the migrant labourers households and blocks. The study has observed the individual workers out-migration on their own without the agents support on bondage of advance may minimise the evils of dadan system but cannot substitute it. The push factors are more stranger, than the pull factors in causing out-migration. Whatever little role the pull factors play they are observable as motivations only for the first experience of the dadan labourers. The study has further, remarked that "the legal measures taken by the Government to regulate the dadan system so as to bring relief to the out-migrants in the event of exploitation could not be realised because of the in-build snags in the law which has given rise to the clandestine drafting and trafficking of dadan labourers."

However, this study had not covered the Surat labourers which is found predominantly in the village of Ganjam, (Orissa).

Joshi (1989)[33] has made a research study on the basis of field work carried out in the city of Raichur of Karnataka State, from the 300 sample families, relating to occupational mobility of migrant labourers. The findings of the study revealed that the middle caste and middle class respondents are more mobile than the other caste and class respondents.

The study further, reveals that although under the impact of urbanisation and industrialisation both migration and mobility have increased they have not redistributed the people into places and positions in an effective way. As a result, higher caste and upper class people are migrating in large proportions to the cities and are employed in urban - occupations. Among the factors contributing to the increasing degree of migration and mobility the caste, class and the kinship factors appear to be more important. The study concluded that factors appear to be more important. The study concluded that neither migration of people to the city nor the occupational mobility of such migrant has affected the basic feature(s) of the Indian society and the urban social structure remains even to-day unaltered in any of its structural aspects.

B.R.K. Raju (1989)[34] conducted a study in the state of Andhra Pradesh in the district of West Godavari, where migrant labourers employed in Tungabhadra Project in Karnataka State. The author's focus on the migration adjustment process at destination and upon return migration are noteworthy aspects. Because of migration to Tungabhadra region, the economic condition of migrants improved considerably. The author concluded that the purpose of such migration was for their economic betterment but due to agonising the lives of millions are more frequently demonstrated, "abject poverty". The author has rightly remarked at the beginning of the book, "In the context of the green revolution, we witness to-day a new phenomenon of surplus labour from the rural areas of neighbouring states reaching various places which have witnessed tremendous rural prosperity. It is this type of rural to rural migration and remittance from one area to another which is a new development on migration "Scene". However, such developmental migration are taking place in a small scale at some localised areas. But massive poverty syndromed labour migration.

The labour Directorate, Orissa have studied (1989)[35] rather surveyed the magnitude of out migrants confining to 'Dadan' labourers in two districts, viz. Ganjam and Puri. But no adequate light has been shed on the basis of empirical studies on socio-economic profile of such families which form the basis of such dadan labourers. Consequently the study could not provide the background data required for further analysis of the economic consequences of migration.

Gupta (1990)[36] in his study examined the migratory process of farm labour in the context of their socio-economic characteristics, factors of migration, method of recruitment and relative deprivation in the agriculturally advanced state of Punjab.

Kasar (1992)[37] has analysed seasonal migration of farm labourers from dry and backward tracts of Maharashtra to co-operative units in irrigation sector for employment and income earning. He has identified the vital factors behind the process of seasonal migration, engaged in harvesting and transport of sugarcane during crushing season of Sugar factories. This seasonal migration has depended upon the involvement of middlemen who generally exploit poor, illiterate and fragmented agricultural labourers. The problems are further aggravated by involvement of women and children who are deprived of the basic facilities of education and health. Hence, the study has significance in view of examining the socio-economic features, made of seasonal migration and its effects on economy of migrant labour. The seasonal migration has significant effect on the annual gross family employment of migrant households, migrants were more indebted than the non-migrants.

The inadequate income and employment opportunities at the place of origin served as push factors for the migrants. On the contrary, the guaranteed employment with high wages for human labour and the availability of green fodder, free charge for animals at the sugar factories served as the pull factors for the seasonal migration of farm labour force the area of origin.

An ICSSR[38] study conducted by Dr. Damodar Panda (1992) has focused light in Inter-country colonial migration, Intra-country colonial migration and Inter-state migration in India with reference to Orissa. The study has critically examined the legal provision protecting the migrant workman. Thus the work is dealt with historical analysis of labour migration alongwith level framework. But no in-depth study of socio-economic problems of migrant workmen has been attempted with statistical technique nor a strategy for combating the problem of Inter-State migrant workmen has been advanced.

An ICSSR supported institution (NICC Centre for Development studies) conducted a study (1993)[39] on dadan migrants, basing on the theme, "the socio-economic study of migrant labour (dadan) from Orissa and the reasons for their migration covering two costal districts viz. Ganjam and Puri. This study has ignored in presenting a total picture of various types of migrant workmen manifested in the state of Orissa.

Barik (1994)[40] has attempted to confine his study on the conditions of surat Oriya migrants, working in the textile factories. The study on the basis of questionnaire and interview method endeavoured to present the structure of art silk Industries, working environment and working conditions and other features of Oriya migrants in Surat. The study also attempts to establish the role of kingship and primordial loyalties in the cycle of migration process.

It also demonstrates the working class consciousness of migrant labourers and their over all economic development. However, Dr. Bark's work has touched as said earlier, only one segment of migrant labourers the other types of migrants like the dadan or other inter-state migrants are not included in the purview of his study.

Thus, there is no paucity of research studies on the problems of labour migration, as has been presented in the proceeding pages by various authors, researchers and many others* which through light on various aspects of migrant labourers in various parts of India. However, studies in the state of Orissa are limited. Unfortunately, mostly studies have been confined to dadan out-migrants only and thereby, no study has been conducted covering all types of migrant workmen i.e. the total out-migration problem.

In view of the above consideration, a study in Ganjam district making a comparative analysis of migrant and non migrants seem highly

---

* i) Premi, Mahendra K. *Urban out-migration : A Study of its nature, cause and consequences*, Sterling Publisher Pvt. Ltd. New Delhi (1980)

ii) Mandal B.R. (Ed.) *Frontiers on Migration Analysis*, Concept publishing company, New Delhi (1981).

iii) Khan, Nijam. *Studies in Human migration*, Rajesh Publication, New Delhi (1983).

iv) Bhandari, S.A. *Study of Pattern and problems of migration of tribal women workers*. ICSSR Project (1990).

v) Koteshewar, R.K. and Joshi, A.S. *Some characteristics of out migration from three types of developing villages in Eastern, Uttar Pradesh.* Journal of Institute of Economic Research, 25 (1-2) January-July 1990.

vi) Mehta, G.S. *Characteristics and Economic implications of migration*, Journal of Rural development 10(6) November, 1991.

vii) Gupta, A.K. *Migration of Agricultural labourers from Eastern to North western region*, Social Change 21(3) Sept., 1991.

imperative.

References

1. Sen, Sukomal. Working class of India (History of Emergence and Movement 1830-1970) K.P. Bagchi and Company, Calcutta, p. 53.

2. Ibid. p.30.

3. Ibid. p. 53

4. Saha, Panchanan. "Emigration of Indian Labour (1834-1900). Peoples Publishing House Pvt. Ltd. , New Delhi, 1970, p. 29.

5. Ibid. p. 31.

6. The famine Commission (1880) and the census Report 1901, pp. 85-85.

7. Ray, S.C. Agricultural indebtedness in India and its remedies. Calcutta University, 1918.

   Extracts from famine commission Report 1880 on the census of and remedies for agricultural indebtedness Part-II, Chapter III, Section IV.

8. Report of the Royal Commission on Labour in India, Agricole Publishing Academy Reprinted 1983. pp. 14-15.

9. Agricultural Labour enquiry, Agricultural wages in India, Delhi (1952), p. 140.

   Rs. 1-8 means Rs. 1 and 8 Anna and Rs. 1-4 means Rs. 1 and 4 anna (Rs. 1 =16 Anna).

10. Tripathy, S.N. "Bonded Labour in India" Discovery Publishing House, New Delhi, 1989, p. 15.

11. Stricken Kalahandi - Commission confirms death

    Frontline, September 28 October 11, 1991, pp. 112-113

    A retired district judge Mr. B.N. Mishra was appointed to prove into the report in a Bhubaneswar based English daily that poverty - stricken tribals of Kalahandi have been dying of starvation. After on investigation in Kalahandi and Bolangir Mishra has confirmed the fact.

12. Desai, A.R. Tribes in Transition p. 510

13. Saha, Panchanan. Op. cit. p. 39.

14. Tripathy, S.N. & Das Sandamini. Informal women labour in India, Discovery Publishing House, New Delhi, 1991, p. 14

15. Senapati, Nilamani (Ed.). Orissa District Gazetteers 1968, Bolangir Chapter XVII, p. 466.

16. Inter-state migrant workmen's (Regulation of Employment and condition of Service) Act, 1979.

The contract Labour (Regulation and Abolition Act) 1970. Minimum Wages Act, 1948, Equal Remuneration Act, 1976 workmen compensation Act, 1923 and the like.

17. Davis, Kingstey. The population of India and Pakistan, Newyork, Princeton University Press (1951).

18. Prabhu, P.N. A study on the social effects of urbanisation of Industrial workers unigrating from rural areas to the city of Bombay, UNESCO Research centre, Calcutta 1956, p. 63.

19. Sovani, N.V. Potential out-migrants and Removal of surplus population in three districts of Orissa (India) Proceedings of the international conference, Vianna, 1959, pp. 703-709.

20. Zachariah, K.C. A historical study of International Migration in the Indian Sub-continent 1901-1931. London, Asia Publishing House, 1964.

21. M.V. George. Internal migration in Assam and Bengal 1901-61 (Unpublished thesis) Australian National Library, Canberra.

22. Vaid, K.N. The New worker, New Delhi, Sri Ram centre for Industrial Relations 1968 pp. 170-172 and 181.

23. National Commission on labour (1969).

24. Saha, Panchanan. Emigration of Indian Labour, People's Publishing House, New Delhi (1970).

25. Srivastav and Ali. Frontiers in migration Analysis, Concept publishing company, New Delhi (1981)

26. Kamble, N.D. Labour migration in Indian States, Ashish Publishing House, New Delhi (1983).

27. Breman, Jan. Of peasants, migrants and pampers: Rural labour circulation in West India, Oxford University Press, New Delhi (1985)

28. Singh, J.P. Pattern of Rural - Urban migration of India, Inter-India Publication, New Delhi (1986).

29. Khan, Nijam. Pattern of Rural out-migration—A Micro level study, B.R. Publishing Corporation, Delhi, (1986).

30. Joshi, Vidut (Ed.). Migrant labour and related issues, Oxford and IBH Publishing Co. Pvt. Ltd., New Delhi (1987).

31. Subrahmanya, R.K.A. Policy and Administration aspects of labour migration in "Migrant labour and Related issues" opp. cit.,

32. Rath, Gopal C; Patra, G.C.; Parida, S.C. Dadan System of out-migration in Orissa: Prachi Prakashan, New Delhi 1989.

33. Joshi, K.G. Migration and Mobility, Himalaya Publishing House, Bombay (1989)

34. Raju, B.R.K. Development migration : A Professional Analysis of Inter-state Rural—Rural migration, Concept Publishing Co. New Delhi (1989).

35. A study of the problems and prospects of migrant workmen of Ganjam and Puri districts. Conducted by the Labour Directorate, Orissa, Bhubaneswar (1989).

36. Gupta, A.K. Sociological Implication of Rural to Rural migration: A case study of Rural Immigrants in Punjab, Vohra Publishers and Distributors Allahabad (1990).

37. Kasar, D.V. Economics of seasonal migration, Classical Publishing Company, New Delhi (1992).

38. Panda, Damodar. Migrant workmen: A socio-legal study, ICSSR Project, 1992.

39. Socio-Economic study of migrant labour (Dadan) from Orissa ICSSR Project, NKC Centre for Development Studies, Bhubaneswar, 1993.

40. Barik, B.C. Rural Migrants in an Urban setting : A case study, Classical Publishing House, Delhi (1994).

2

Problems of Migrant Workmen in Orissa

This chapter illustrates some problems of migrant workmen with the help of secondary sources of data. Besides, the main features of Inter-state Migrant Workmen Act, 1979 has been examined, keeping in view the problems of migrant labourers.

Studies on Migrant Labour in Orissa

The plights and problems of migrant labourers have in recent years, caught the attention of the researchers, social workers, media personalities, courts and of course Government. Social workers have raised their concern about the exploitation and miserable plight of the migrant labourers.

Despite deep concern over the issue of migrant labour, no reliable data are available with regard to magnitude and size of the migrant workmen in the state of Orissa. Studies conducted by labour Directorate, Orissa on the basis of complaints received, investigations made and enquiries conducted estimated the size of migrant Dadan labour from Orissa during 1988. The figure revealed at about 1.5 lakhs every year pertaining to dadan labour only. But the incidence of migrant labour in Orissa is vast and extensive at it embraces various categories of migrant labour including Surat and Other migrants.

The Centre of Regional Studies, Utkal University estimated that "nearly 2 Lakh labourers of the state migrate seasonally to other states for wages as dadan labourers."

1. Research Study by Directorate of Labour and Labour Welfare Department

A joint study conducted by the Directorate of Labour Orissa and Labour Welfare department, Utkal University has brought to light the following important findings:

i) About 93 percent of the migrant labourers belonged to the economically weaker sections of the society. Twenty six percent being scheduled castes and scheduled tribes population.

ii) Wide-spread poverty, lack of alternative employment, lack of irrigation facilities compelled these migrant labourers to migrate to other states.

iii) Ninety six percent of them are indebted.

iv) Sixty six percent of them are illiterate, thirty one percent of them read up to class-IV and the remaining three percent read upto class IX.

v) The contractors and agents of the locality having much influence in the area were mainly responsible for their drafting to different states.

vi) Sixty-six percent to Dadan Labourers received their wages and the remaining 34 percent of them lost a part of their wages due to the mischief of the local agents and Khaladars.

vii) The landless proletariat being unable to get the benefit of loan from the nationalized banks approach to the money lenders for loan to meet their social exigencies.

viii) The Inter-state migrant workmen Act 1979 was just enforced in the state. There was no exclusive machinery in the state labour Directorate to enforce the law.

ix) Security bottleneck was the main bottle-neck for registration of contractors/agents.

2. Dadan System of Out-migration in Orissa (ICSSR Sponsored Project)—1987-88.

The Industrial Relations and Personnel Management Department of Berhampur University conducted this project work in 12 villages in the district of Ganjam. The report also highlighted the condition of migrant workmen working in Tehri Dam Project in the State of Uttar Pradesh. This survey also disclosed identical socio-economic conditions of migrant workmen and their plights in the hands of unscrupulous contractors. Among others, the project report said to have commented that the Inter State Migrant Workmen (RECS) Act, 1979 is rendundant since clandestine recruitment and so motto migration do not cover under this. Besides there is no legal bar to check the dadan labourers, who run away from the midway after receipt to due advance.

3. Socio-Economic Conditions of Dadan Labourers 1987–88

The Centre of Regional Studies, Utkal University, Bhubaneswar also conducted a pilot study on the socio-economic condition of Dadan labourers in 16 dadan labour house holds in the district of Puri, Brief disclosures of the report are as follows :-

"Owing to illiteracy and poverty, the Dadan Labourers were being exploited by the Agent who recruited them. They had not bargaining power to settle the wages, duration of work-hours etc. They were being less fed and less paid by the Agents. They were being tortured at work site, made to work for longer hours and forced to remain to unhygenic conditions.

Generally weaker sections of the community were forced to migrate because of the pressure on the land holding. Illiteracy constitute 61.65% of the total dadan labour population. The average monthly income of inter-state migrant workmen was 564.00. They were mostly indebted on account of social customs in the family and they incurred loan mostly from the money lenders at an exorbitant rate of interest i.e. 5 paise per rupee per month which comes to 60% per annum. The socio-economic conditions of inter country migrant workmen was slightly better as revealed from this study. There, the main aim of the people was to make money and invest them in profit yielding enterprises to improve their economic condition.

"The analysis of socio-economic condition of Inter-State Migrant Workmen reveal that they mostly suffer from illiteracy and poverty. Maintenance of family with law per capita income compels them incur loan from money lenders. Under these situations, for maintenance of family and repayment of family borrowings, they are forced to go on Dadan. Thus, the factors responsible are leading one to Inter-State Migration on Dadan are more economic than social."

The Labourers are mostly self motivated to go on dadan and it is not a new thing for them. But for 50 years or so members of these house-holds have been going on dadan. They usually migrate on dadan for 3 to 5 month a year. This dadan helps them in two ways. First, they get some advance from the agents which helps them to maintain their families during slack season, and their period of absence. Secondly, 3 to 5 months continuous wage is assured.

The Dadan labourers are accommodated in special built huts/sheds and are provided with light and drinking water facilities.

The Dadan Labourers generally perform earth work and concrete work. They generally work 9 to 10 hours a day and they are paid over-time wages beyond ten hours a day. They get rice and ration worth Rs. 5/- a day. In case of illness they are supplied with free medicines and if the illness prolongs they are sent back to their villages with all dues payable to them. But when a labour returns back before completing the contract period he is not paid his return fare. But in other cases, return journey expenses are borne by the Contractors/Agents.

The Dadan labourers being illiterate are not aware of the laws regulating the Dadan Labour. Before leaving for workplace they sign the agreement form without knowing the contents in it.

The workers contacted in the study did not reveal their dissatisfaction either with the work or with the agents and the employer.

The study concluded that "unless the economic conditions of these persons improve and are provided with alternative sources of employment suitable to their requirements to local areas the system of Dadan will continue to operate. Instead of trying to discourage the system through legislative measures, it would be more appropriate, if positive measures are taken to improve their working conditions. After all, most of the persons who are going as dadan are in favour of its continuance."

4. Study Conducted by the Authors Relating to Migrant Child Labourers in Orissa (1996–97)

Though the study was aimed at examining the living conditions of migrant child labourers of Bolangir and Surat migrant child labourers of Ganjam, some meaningful conclusions have arrived at with regard to migrant labourers of Bolangir and Ganjam Districts of Orissa.

Migrant labourers are mainly from the scheduled castes, scheduled tribes and backward communities of drought-prone regions of Patnagarh, Belpara, Khaparakhol, Turukela Blocks of Bolangir Districts.

A close observation of Bolangir migrant labourers and that of Ganjam District confirms to the fact that the former are relatively deprived of basic necessities and struggle for their existence. The consumption pattern, land-holding, asset position, level of education, extent of indebtedness etc. clearly reveal that migrant labourers of Ganjam are better off. Some of the migrant households migrate for better prospects of income in the place of destination compared to the place of Ganjam District. But all most all migrant households of Bolangir are belonging to the most deplorable, deprived sections of the society.

These studies in general brought to light the following inferences:

The emergence of labour migration owes its origin from assetlessness and landlessness of parents, distressed living conditions, indebtedness and bondage etc.

Unequal wealth and income distribution, scanty resource flow to rural areas for employment generation and agricultural development etc. have added fuel to the fire of the problem of migration.

Changes in the socio-economic scenario like rapid urbanization, disintegration of joint family and community structure have exerted influence for accelerating the migration process.

The phenomenon of rural-urban migration, must be viewed in the light of prevailing rural conditions of poverty, inequality and unemployment which the socio-economic policies of the Government could not able to mitigate. Economic factors in all migration streams from rural India. Economic hardships emerge from numerous causes. Over population with a proportionate expansion of economic avenues of employment and the reluctant stagnation leads to abject poverty.

Rural conditions are undoubtedly deplorable but these are not the only dominant factors of all rural urban- migration.

Rapid growth of population, increased pressure and over crowdedness in agriculture, decline in cottage industries and handicrafts etc. resulted in uneconomic holdings, unemployment, and migration of labourers.

The accumulated debt, high rent, failure of crops due to uncertain rainfalls and drought leads to precarious living standard of agricultural labourers. This has induced a continual exodus of rural population into urban areas in search of employment, better wages and higher standard of living. The problems of migrant labourers are not to be isolated from the problems of unemployment, poverty and indebtedness. Thus, the problem has its ramifications in the totality of the problem of poverty and unemployment.

Measures to ameliorate the problems of unemployment in the drought-prone districts of Bolangir, Kalahandi and the tribal pockets of Ganjam have remained elusive.

In the following paragraphs, we may briefly, therefore, recapitulate the nature of the existing problems so that solutions sought to the problems of migrant labourers genuinely address themselves to the basic issues of unemployment and poverty.

So for as secondary sources of data available relating to the problems of migrant workmen, the problem of dadan labour has been well-document and high-lighted by the labour Directorate, Orissa.

Problems of Migrant Workmen

Problems of migrant workmen are manifold. These problems may be classified into two; (1) the plight of migrant workmen at the time of recruitment and at the work sites and (2) the problems arising out of the difficulties experienced in administration and implementation of the Inter State Migrant workmen (RECS) Act, 1979. These are dealt in detail as follows. Problems at the time of recruitment and plight of migrant workmen at the work sites are being reflected in different medias more particularly in news papers, review reports, investigations and study reports. Both the administrative machinery while investigating into the complaints inside and outside the state and the voluntary agencies, journalists come across such horrifying stories relating to the plights of migrant workmen. They may be summed up as follows.

a) Clandestine Recruitment

Freedom of movement and freedom to choose one's avocation is one of the constitutional rights guaranteed by the Constitution of India. If an adult workmen voluntarily wants to go to another State in search of employment, it is not possible to check him to do so and he cannot be compelled to disclose his destination and the names of the agents and contractors who is responsible for his drafting. Therefore, clandestine movement of migrant labourers from this state to outside the State is continuing unabated. Besides, if he is a Hindu he says that he is going for pilgrimage either to the holy river Ganges or Badrinath or the like. If he is a Muslim he confesses that he has come out for Mecca or Madina. If he is an adolescent he very quickly replies that he is in a pleasure trip mission for sight seeing. But, this is not their inner voice, rather they are compelled to outburst this as they may not be allowed to be boarded in the train by the agent on his expenses to the work site. The poor labourer only with the fear of loosing his bread conceals his real intention and destination.

b) High Hopes and High Ambitions

The agent and contractors deploy their Khatadars and Dalalas in the drought hitted areas and lure the young and able bodied persons to go to outside the State for employment with higher wages and better living conditions. The youngsters are also being tempted for sight seeing. But the contractors seldom keep up their promises and exploit the poor migrant workmen for their innocence and lack of organisation among the rank and file.

But the question arises, if it a fact, how lakhs of migrant labourer migrant every year from the same are, same village and same family? Poverty is not the only answer to such a question. There are other reasons too. Firstly, during off season, there is no other avenues of employment in the un-irrigated areas. Secondly, all the contractors are not un-scrupulous and through generations they are in the profession and victimization may be a rare phenomenon.

Thirdly, even the matriculates, under matrices prefer to go to outside the state rather work in their fields as matter of prestige. (This was disclosed by two youngsters in course of an interview with the migrant workmen in a training camp organised by the Labour Directorate at Ghatgaon, Keonjhar. They said further that no body will know that what they are doing. Outside employment will fetch them good bride and lumpsum dowry). Fourthly, no able bodied youth (especially of Ghumsar and Khurdha Sub-divisions) prefer to sit in idleness without any work. By tradition they are hard working and prepared to face challenges. Last but not the least they are being lured by their-co-workers who had the long years of experience in visiting other State as dadan labourers. Hence they migrate on account of socio-economic reasons. Moreover, in reality no good contractor keeps up his promise to the fullest extent, the workers either partly or fully loose their legitimate claims. The most attractive offer is the payment of advance at the time of recruitment besides supply of food and journey expenses by the agents and contractors. Thus this system has grown out of the very name' Dadan' which refers payment of advance at the time of recruitment.

c) Longer Hours of Work and Low wages

At the work site it is alleged that the migrant workmen are compelled to work for 14 to 16 hours a day with nominal food and without extra wages. This is also partly true. Since the dadan labourers of orissa mostly prefer to work on piece rate basis, there is no hard and first rule for such longer hours of work in actual practice and for better wages even the workers prefer to work in the moonlit night and or in the odd hours. Besides in cold climate working for 8 to 10 hours of a day is not a problem for the Oriya migrant workmen who are well accustomed to work for six to eight hours a day under the hot sun in their native land. But there daily wages are paid on the time rate basis, there the dadan labourers are denied of their over time wages and off day wages and they are asked to work more than eight hours a day and in certain cases longer hours of work are extracted under compelling circumstances. But, in any case wages are not low as compared to the wages in the home land of dadan labourers. There are instances of payment of lower wages to the dadan labourer as compared to their counter part in the recipient States.

d) Dadan Labourers are Kept in Cages

In 1985, such a horrifying story was published in the leading dailies of the countries and that attracted the attention of the State Government in October 1985 when the Orissa Govt. was made to understand that thousands of oriya migrant labourers were compelled to work in most in-human conditions, workers are kept in cages, they are given the kind of food and water that the animal may hesitate to take and workers unwilling to work and want to run away from the work site were pitched in the river Bhagirathi where the Tehri Dam was being constructed in the Himalayas. On receipt of the information a team of Officers of the State Labour

Directorate rushed to the spot and investigated into the complaint.

The observation of the team regarding the alleged atrocities is summed up as follows :

i) That total number of Oriya migrant workmen in the two Projects i.e. Maneri Bhalli Hydro Electric Project Stage-II (ii) Tehri Dam Project of Uttarkashi and Tehri Garwal Districts is estimated at 839.

ii) None wanted to come back notwithstanding assistance and assurance for safe return. Some volunteered to say that workmen, on the whole, are happy and contended.

iii) In the matter of implementation of the Inter State Migrant workmen (R.E. & C.S), Act, 1979 and Rules the followings were observed.

a) Licences granted and valid upto 31.12.84 have not been renewed for the year 1985. Recruitment/employing agents are operating without having licence. (Details are available in the report).

b) The present minimum rate of wages comprising of basic and D.A. is Rs. 16.80 per day for an unskilled worker. The statutory right of the employee is to receive wages at the rate not lower than the notified minimum rate. Documentary evidences show payment of minimum wages to the workers. Lack of evidence and absence of complaint are the major constraints to proceed against the erring agents/contractors. Contractors beat their own drums contending that they are paying notified wages and commission @ of 8 to 10% of total wages to the agents. Surprisingly enough, they do not seemingly bother about actual payment of proper wages to workers or otherwise, thereby leaving the workmen at the mercy of agents.

c) Delay in payment of monthly wages particularly in M/s. N.P.C.C. at Tehri came to the notice of the team.

d) Workers are made to work beyond 48 hours in a week for which payment is not made at the prescribed rate. This by and large, depends upon the statement/ evidence of the workers concerned.

e) The team visited the Camps and found that the Oriya migrant workmen are kept in covered tin-sheds. Some companies have very recently provided wooden planks and rope-cots.

f) No latrine, urinal and bathroom have been provided at the camps.

g) Medical facilities provided are inadequate.

h) No protective clothing has been supplied with the on-set of the of winter which is severe in those hilly areas. Only two days ago, M/s. Continental Construction (P) Ltd. at Joshiyara have provided blankets to the migrant workmen.

i) Wholesome drinking water has not been provided at Joshiyara and Dharasu Camps. But the position can not be said to be unsatisfactory at Tehri.

j) Contractors are very much luke-warm to the idea of elimination of middle-men, although they are equally accountable to the migrant workmen for all purposes.

k) Both the principal employer and contractors are indifferent to their statutory obligation towards migrant workmen. There has been virtually no attempt on the part of the principal employer i.e. officials of I & P Deptt. of Uttar Pradesh to discharge their legal responsibilities. Payment of proper wages to the migrant workmen calls for a high degree of vigilance of the principal employers and this is the duty which they owe to workers.

l) Taking into account the totality of the situation, the conditions of Oriya migrant workmen have shown marked improvement. Excepting some irregularities/lapses as observed, there have been no complaints of major violations from the workers during the visit of the team.

m) Critics are very vociferous abut the plight of migrant workmen of which they know very little relating to actual state of affairs.

*e) Non-payment of Wages/less Payment of Wages and Repatriation**

The statement given below will indicate the nature of complaints

*For details kindly refer to "A Study of the Problems and Prospects of Migrant Workmen of Ganjam and Puri" Districts, Labour Directorate, Orissa.

investigated by the Officers of the Labour Directorate in different State from 1980 to 1988.

Sl. No.	*Year*	*No. of Officer*	*Name of the State and Place of Inquiry*	*Summary of the Findings*
1.	June, 80	1 (One)	NPCC Ltd., Srugane, Chhamba, H.P.	Arranged return of 22 migrant workmen with wages.
2.	Feb. 81	1 (One)	NTPC, Korba, M.P.	Arranged return of 172 migrant workmen with wages.
3.	April, 81	1 (One)	Md. Quam Nizami Kisti Wad, J & K	Arranged return of 24 migrant workmen with wages.
4.	July, 81	1 (One)	SMT Pvt. Ltd., Murdeswar, Karnatak.	Arranged return of 23 migrant workmen with wages.
5.	Nov. 81	1 (One)	Gauhati, Assam	Arranged return of 21 migrant workmen with wages.
6.	Jan. 81	1 (One) A.L.C., Orissa posted at New Delhi inquired in different States from time to time and arranged return of workers	Jammu & Kashmir	Arranged return of 22 migrant workmen with wages.
7.	Jan. 81	—do—	Ghajiabad, U.P.	Arranged return of 2 migrant workmen with wages.
	—do—	—do—	Chandighat, Hardwar, U.P	Arranged return of 4 migrant workmen with wages.
	—do—	—do—	Khara, Dehradun, U.P	Arranged return of 14 migrant workmen with wages.
8.	July, 82	A.L.C., Orissa posted at New Delhi enquired in different Sta-	Hapur, U.P.	Arranged return of 14 migrant workmen with wages.

(Contd.)

Sl. No.	*Year*	*No. of Officer*	*Name of the State and Place of Inquiry*	*Summary of the Findings*
		tes from time to time & arranged return of workers		
9.	Jan. 82	—do—	Ghungural, Ghaziabad, U.P.	Arranged return of 1 migrant workmen with wages.
10.	Sept. 82	2 (Two)	Hyderabad, Yerraguntals Cuddapat, A.P.	Officers were entrusted the work of enumuration of migrant labourers of Orissa. No complaint from the migrant workmen working was received by the enquiring Officers regarding their safe-return to their home except the over-time wages, Holidays proper medical facilities. The enquiring officers brought the above complaints to the notice of the concerned Labour Commissioner who are competent as per the Sec. 13, 14, 15, 16 & 17 of I.B.M.W. (R & E & CS) Act for ensuring such provisions of law.
	Sept. 82	2 (Two)	Narayanpur, Ghataprava, Karnatak.	—do—
	—do—	2 (Two)	Hoogly, Howrah, W.B.	—do—
	—do—	2 (Two)	1) Bhatsanagar, Taluk Dist. Thane Maharastra. 2) Tata Electrical Company Unit-5 500 M.W. Bombay Maharastra.	—do—

(Contd.)

Sl. No.	*Year*	*No. of Officer*	*Name of the State and Place of Inquiry*	*Summary of the Findings*
	—do—	A.L.C., Orissa posted at New Delhi enquired in different States from time to time and arranged return of workers	Hazra Fertilizer Wanskberi, Gujarat.	—do—
	—do—	2(Two)	1) Wrangehu, Assam	—do—
	—do—	2 (Two)	2) Shillong, Meghalaya	—do—
9.	Dec. 83	1 (One)	Brick Field, Calcutta W.B. Hindustan Paper Corpn. Jugi Road, Assam, Garampani Amthring Assam, Shillong, Meghalaya, Langpt, Project, Assam.	
10.	Mar., 83	1 (One)	Sanguam, Goa	Arranged return of 11 migrant workmen with wages.
11.	Feb. 85	2 (Two)	Vizagnatnam Steel Plant At-Balacharuvu, A.P.	No complaint has been received from the workmen at the time of inquiry regarding their return to home.
12.	Oct. 85	5 (Five)	Tehri garwal and Uttar Kanshi, U.P.	The workmen who were working at the time of inquiry, were reluctant to come back home.
13.	Mar. 86	1 (One)	Visakhapatnam Steel Plant, A.P.	—do—
14.	19.3.86	1 (One)	Salalal Project Dhyangarh, J & K	—do—

(Contd.)

Sl. No.	*Year*	*No. of Officer*	*Name of the State and Place of Inquiry*	*Summary of the Findings*
15.	Mar. 86	1 (One)	Subarnarekha Dam Works At/PO : Chandili, Dist. Singhbhumi, Bihar	Sri H. Khan, Asst. Labour Officer has left for Bihar for inquiry and repatriation of workmen and repatriated the alleged workmen.
16.	Mar. 86	1 (One)	U.P. State Bridge Corporation At/PO; Chachai, Dist. Rewa	Sri P.K. Jena, ALO has been ordered to enquire in M.P. and arrange repatriation of migrant workers with payment of arrear wages to the tune of about Rs. two lakhs.
17.	1987	7	Assam, Jammu & Kashmir, Uttar Pradesh, Gujarat and West Bengal.	Arranged return of 126 workers and realised arrear wages to the tune of Rs. 38,343.00
18.	1988	6	Uttar Pradesh, Assam, Meghalaya and Punjab.	Repatriated 200 migrant workmen and realised and disbursed arrear wages of Rs. 1,09,198.00.

The statement indicates the following position with regard to repatriation of dadam labourers and non-payment or less payment of their wages.

a) The dadan labourers are denied of their assured wages.

b) They are detained by the contractors for longer period over and above the oral contract entered into between the parties.

c) The State Government of other States could not detect such violations in course of their regular inspections of their Labour Enforcement Machineries partly due to language gap and partly due to concealing of records by the agents and Khatadars whose accounts are seldom borne in the records of the respective State Governments.

(f) Difficulties experienced in administration and implementation of the Inter State Migrant Workmen (RE &CS) Act, 1979.

1) The amount prescribed for security deposit is very high and no agent

is coming forward to invest such a huge amount of money to obtain a licence.

2) Despite specific provisions made in Sub-Sec. (3) of Section 20 of the aforesaid Act, the Government of the States where the Migrant workers of Orissa re-going to work, have not declared the officers of this Directorate as Inspectors under the aforesaid Act for facilitating quick implementation of the provisions of the said Act although repeated correspondences have been made with the other State Governments on this score. This is very much necessary because the migrant workers of this State who are going to work in other States seldom know any language other than Oriya besides being un-organised.

3) Non-framing and notifying the Rules by some State Government/ Union Territories.

4) Not taking action against the Contractors/Principal Employer by the recipient states for entertainment of migrant labour without obtaining licence from the prescribed authority of the home State of the workmen.

5) The Principal employers of other state are not issuing certificates in the prescribed manner as required in sub-Rule (3) of Rule-7 of the Orissa Rules and absence of a certificate is creating difficulties for issue of a licence to the contractor.

6) Extreme poverty, illiteracy, socio-economic backwardness, lack of organisation and the consequential lack of the ability to collective bargain among the Inter State Migrant Workmen leading to denial of the statutory benefits to them.

7) A case under the Workmens' Compensation Act relating to the compensation payable to a deceased/injured migrant workmen cannot be transferred to his home State unless all the parties to the proceedings agree to such transfer as required in proviso to Subsection (2) of Sec. 21 of the Workmens' Compensation Act. The employers in the State where the migrant workers are dying or sustaining injuries through accidents arising out of and in course of employment are not agreeing to the transfer of the compensation cases contested by them to the home state of the deceased/injured

workmen. This provision of law should be amended and the employer in the outside State in such a case should be legally compelled to attend the Courts in home State of the deceased/injured workman for adjudication in the compensation cases wherever necessary. Such an amendment of the Act is desirable as financially the workman is unable to do so compared to his employer.

Information received by the State Labour Directorate reveal that 214 migrant workmen died in course of employment and an amount of Rs. 1620708/- has been disbursed as compensation.

In this context, it is mention-worthy regarding the evaluation of measures undertaken by the labour Directorate, Orissa by undertaking series of conferences to arrive at meaningful solutions to the emerging and serious problem of migrant workmen in the state of Orissa.

The organisation, discussion and deliberation of the conferences have been out-lined in the following paragraphs.

Labour Ministers' Conference and their Recommendations on Migrant Labour

The 33rd session of the State Labour Ministers' conference was held on 16th Sept. 1982 at New Delhi. It discussed inter-alia, the problem of migrant workmen and arrived at the following conclusions.

The State Labour Ministers/Representatives of other States indicated the steps taken in their respective States with regard to the implementation of the Inter State Migrant Workers' Act. The conference agreed that the difficulties coming in the way of problems of Migrant labourers from one State to another should be identified by the concerned State Govts. by mutual discussion and if necessary, by a joint study.

In this connection, the conference concluded that there was already a proposal to have two study groups to examine the difficulties of the migrant workmen, one covering the labourers migrating from Bihar, Orissa and Rajasthan to Punjab, Haryana, Delhi, Himachal Pradesh and Jammu and Kashmir and the other in respect of the labourers migrating from Andhra Pradesh to Maharashtra.

The Conference emphasized the urgent need on the framing and notification of the rules under the Inter State Migrant Workmen (Regulation of Employment and Condition of Service) Act, 1979 by all these State Governments who have not yet done so and implement the same without further delay.

Suggestion were also given by Labour Minister of Orissa covering the need for amendment to section 21 of the workmens' Compensation Act, 1923 for transferring the claim of migrants to the native States for issue of award and payment of compensation to the legal heirs of a deceased workman, adequate police help for all the enquiring officers, associating voluntary organisations for educating the migrant workers, etc. A point was also made that since some of the State have not yet appointment registering and licensing officers, the Central Government may take steps for appointment of registering and licensing officers irrespective of the fact whether the Central Government is the appropriate Government or not.

The conference also endorsed all the recommendations of the working group.

The Chairman assured the State that all the suggestions would be carefully considered for taking appropriate action by the Centre.

7. Joint Study Teams

Following the 23rd session of Labour Ministers' Conference, Government of India in their Notification No. UR 3013 (8) 82 LW dated the 5th November, 1982 of the Ministry of Labour and issued the following Resolution which has been published in the Gazette of India extraordinary part, Section 1 Dated the 30th April, 1983.

"Complaints have been received from time to time from Rajasthan, Orissa and Bihar about the unsatisfactory working and living conditions of migrant workers migrating from these States to Delhi, Jammu & Kashmir, Punjab, West Bengal, Madhya Pradesh, Haryana and Himachal Pradesh. Similar difficulties faced by labourers migrating from Andhra Pradesh to Maharashtra particularly to Greater Bombay City area have also been reported. The various problems and difficulties concerning the migrant labour were discussed in a meeting held with Labour Secretaries of 11 States at New Delhi, on the 21st August, 1982, under the Chairmanship of Secretary, Ministry of Labour. It was found that a number of States have not framed and notified the Rules under the Inter State Migrant Workmen (Regulation of Employment and Conditions of Service) Act,

1979 which made the task of enforcement of the provisions of that Act difficult. It was felt that in the meanwhile a Joint Team of officials of the States concerned, i.e. of the State from where the workers migrate and the State to which they migrate, may meet periodically to deal with certain specific aspects of the problems of migrant labour. It was also suggested that joint studies may be carried out on the actual working and living conditions of the migrant workers by visiting the work site to have a first hand knowledge of the working and living conditions and also to deal with specific complaints. Accordingly, it has been decided to constitute joint study teams consisting of the officials of the Central and the State Government concerned.

The joint study team visited different states in order to:

i) visit the work sites of the representative States where migrant workmen are employed and in respect of which specific complaints have been received.

ii) make an on the spot study of the problem of migrant labour with reference to these specific complaints and

iii) carry out general inspection with a view to redressing the other grievances of the migrant workers on the sport, if any (over and above the specific complaints).

Internal migration facilities the process of economic and social development because it contributes to urban growth, provides much of the work-force for industrial expansion, and increasingly permits women to participate in development. It has many other ramifications. However, to extent that rural-urban migrants are better educated and more ambitious that those who do not move, such migration constitutes a drain on useful human resources in rural areas with detrimental effects on rural development.

In certain context, migration could benefit rural areas. Migrants in urban areas may remit sizeable amount of money to their families and relatives in rural areas. This remittance, if utilized for productive investments in agriculture, village industries, animal husbandry may reap immense benefit to the families of migrant workmen. Such, remittance may liquidate the indebted families and may bring the family out of the debt trap.

But the unskilled, illiterate and simple labourers especially from the tribal belts of Orissa are recruited by the contractors, the worst form is the Dadan labourers.

While some workers migrate on the their own, the others are recruited by the contractors/Agents/Sub-Agents/ from one State to work at a work site in another State. The workers who are recruited by the Contractors/Agents/Sub-Agents are given a number of allurements at the time of employment. However, all sorts of promises made at the time of recruitment are not fulfilled and all hopes and expectations are belied once a migrant workman reaches distant place. Taking advantage of the situation, they are mercilessly exploited by way of

a) Denial of minimum wages.

b) Non payment of wages and delayed payment of wages.

c) Arbitrary computation of wages paid in kind cash.

d) Unauthorised deductions from wages as Jamadari Commission (Jamadar is a sub-agent of the Contractor).

e) Denial of payment of journey allowance and displacement allowance.

f) Denial of adequate residential accommodation.

g) Denial of Protective clothing.

h) Denial of adequate first-aid and hospital facilities.

i) Denial of the compensation under the Workmens' compensation Act, 1923 in case of injury/accident or death.

j) Denial of benefits flowing from the Inter-State Migrant Workmen (Regulation of Employment and Conditions of Service) Act, 1979 by taking the plea that they have come on their own to work in other state.

Inspite of all these problems, the migration itself can not be completely ruled out. However, its evil affects can be minimized to a very great extent. In order to ensure better working and living conditions to the migrant labour, the Inter State Migrant Workmen (Regulation of Employment and Conditions of Service) Act, 1979 has been enacted. Although about 18 years have elapsed, enforcement of the statutory provision has been beset with difficulties on account of various factors, e.g.

a) Non-framing and notifying the Rules by a few State Government.

b) Non-appointment of Statutory authorities, such as, Licensing, Registering and Inspecting Authorities.

c) Some of the States not concurring with the proposal for appointment of Inspectors by one State having jurisdiction in another State as required under Section 20(3) of the Act.

d) Want of statistical data about the number of workmen migrating on their own and being recruited through the Agents and Sub-Agents of the Contractors.

e) Extreme poverty, illiteracy, socio-economic backwardness, lack of organisation and the consequential lack of the ability of collective bargain among the inter state migrant workmen leading to denial of the statutory benefits to them.

f) Seasonal and fluctuating nature of employment as in the bricks kilns which makes it difficult enforcing agency to enforce the statutory provisions.

g) Barriers of communication between the employers, the contractors, the Inter-State Migrant workmen and the law enforcing agencies on account of differences of language, customs, practices and procedures followed by the Courts etc.

h) The workers are deprived of various benefits by employers, taking the plea that they are not Inter State Migrant Workmen as defined under the Inter State Migrant Workmen (Regulation of Employment and Conditions, of Service) Act, 1979.

In order to remedy the situation, the following suggestions were made by the Joint Study Team:

1) It is very necessary to identify the migrant labourers. People migrate from a few selected areas of State and not from all the areas. Usually, agricultural labourers migrate from Saharsa, Motihari, Sitamari, Darbhanga, Madhubani, Bhagalpur, Samastipur and West Champaran District of North Bihar, Saharanpur and Ajamgarh Districts in Uttar

Pradesh to Punjab, from Jhabu, Madhya Pradesh to Rajasthan, Puri and Ganjam Districts of Orissa to Punjab, Haryana, Himachal Pradesh, Jammu and Kashmir, Manipur, Tripura, Assam and Meghalaya etc. It is necessary that these areas are identified and statistical data collected about the number of workmen who are migrating on their own or who are being recruited through agents and agents of Contractors, their social and economic background, aptitudes, skills reasons for migration etc. The Labour Department of each state and Union Territories may for this purpose consider opening a cell which will have mobile units to move and collect information about the incidence of migration from different areas.

2) It should be possible to organise mobile teams for checking at the Railway Stations, Bus Stops, Inter-State border check posts etc. about the number of workmen moving from one state to another. Though such a process of identification may not be profit it will give an approximate idea about the extent of migration.

3) After the collection of aforesaid data, establishments where they are employed should be got identified. The various States and Central Government should indicate the large and medium size of the establishments employing migrant labour.

4) The enforcement machinery of the recipient State could write to the originating State after identifying the work sites where Inter-State Migrant Workmen are employed enquiring as to whether the Inter-State Migrant Workmen came on their own or recruited through the Agents.

5) Specific complaints already circulated by the Member Convener amongst the representatives of the various State should be enquired into by Senior Officer of the Labour Department so that remedial measures may be adopted. Hitherto, such complaints have been dismissed as vague and non-specific.

6) Rules relating to the deposit of security money may be amended to specify the amount of security to be deposited by the contractors having regard to his financial conditions.

7) There should be more intensive and extensive enforcement of the Inter-State Migrant Workmen (Regulation of Employment and Con-

ditions of Service) Act, 1979. The defaulting employers should be brought to book and their contracts be cancelled.

8) The definition of the "Inter State Migrant Workmen" should be a amended as to safe-guard the interest of the migrant labour. This would check up the tendency of the employers to evade the provisions of this important piece of legislation.

9) In view of the existing constraints on the inspecting officers, it is suggested that the officers enforcing these labour laws should be provided with a Scooter/Motor Cycle at Government cost. Should this be not possible, the officers may be granted advances to purchase the Scooters which may be recovered in easy instalments and propulsion charges be borne by the Government.

10) The questionnaire already circulated by the Members convener amongst the members of the Joint Study Team should be completed and submitted to the Director Shri Jagdish at a very early date.

11) The Workmens' Compensation Act, 1923 should be amended so as to provide full relief to the migrant workmen and their families, in case of accident or death arising out of the employment and in the course of employment. The enforcement of this piece of legislation has not been proper. In the Central Sphere, the officers have not been appointed as Compensation Commissioner. The Team feels that the Regional Labour Commissioner (Central) should be appointed as Compensation Commissioner which would ensure quick relief to the workers in the Central sphere.

12) The State of Orissa has sent a list of contractors employing migrant workmen in different parts of the country. Such lists should be provided by the State of Bihar, West Bengal, Madhya Pradesh, Uttar Pradesh and Rajasthan. At least two important establishments should visited in each State by the Joint Study Team as a whole to study the working and living conditions of the migrant labour.

13) A Labour Officer or a Welfare Officer should be posted by the State to which the migrant workmen belong at the work site where they are employed to look after their welfare and other amenities.

14) The members from Orissa, Uttar Pradesh, Bihar, Rajasthan and Madhya Pradesh should complete and forward a list of fresh com-

plaints relating to the Inter State Migrant workmen to the Convener so that he in turn could get them sent to different States for immediate necessary follow up section.

15) Payment of Minimum Wages should be ensured at all cost. Besides, minimum wages, minimum basic amenities should be provided at the labour camp: This should include proper water and drainage facilities.

16) Temporary Ration Card should be issued to them to make them entitled to draw their rations from the Fair price shops.

17) A mobile medical unit should be set up at the labour camp.

18) Literacy class should be set up during the period of camp by the Directorate of Central Board for workers education.

19) Creches and Nursery Schooling facilities be provided during the camp.

20) Wherever, rules under Inter State Migrant Workmen (Regulation of Employment and Conditions of Service) Act, 1979 have not been framed should be framed without any further delay. The authorities should also be appointed for immediate enforcement of the Act.

As the Joint Study Team has been constituted only after consultations with and after the approval of the Labour Secretaries, it should function with real and enthusiasm. Once all the State Governments which are represented in the Joint Study Teams start evincing the desired extent of interest in the working of the Joint Study Team, it should be possible for the study team to solve many specific complaints and grievances of Inter State Migrant workmen employed in different projects through a process of the spot study, persuasion and discussions.

Amendment of section 21(2) of the Workmens' compensation Act, 1923, the State Government may like to take advantage of Section 21(5) and may appoint an officer from the originating State as the Commissioner for Workmens' Compensation to hear and decide cases involving payment of compensation to the dependent of the Inter State Migrant Workmen who died or who were disabled (Partially or totally) due to and in the course of employment.

The migrant workmen in the country are in a miserable plight. They leave their families and came for work at a very distant place. We must take very human and sympathetic view of their plight as they have suffered a lot and they have to work in a surrounding, quite different from their socio-economic back ground.

The following important points were kept in view before the enactment of Inter-state Migrant Workmen Act, 1979.

i) The Inter-state migrant workmen belong to the lower state of the society.

ii) The migrant workmen are mostly agricultural labourers. They are illiterate and unable to speak any other language other than Oriya.

iii) Dealing with provisions of labour laws, the court adopts such procedures which become totally unintelligible to such migrant workmen. As a result of which they could not able to get only relief by taking shelter of legal procedure.

iv) In the absence the direct link between the employer and employee relationship, the workmen can only seek assistance through the sub-contractors.

The Inter-state migrant workmen (Regulation of employment condition of service) Act 1979 aims at regulating the employment of Inter-State migrants workmen and providing them conditions of service and for matters connected therewith, The Act seeks to ensure:

i) Registration of all principal employers/contractors and licensing of all contractors employing five or more migrant workmen.

ii) Issue of pass book to every Interstate migrant-workmen indicating the name and the place the establishment where the workmen is employed, the period of employment, the proposed rates and modes of payment of wages and the return and the return fair payable to him on the expiry of the period of his employment or any contingencies, such as resignation or the termination of employment before the expiry of a such period.

iii) Payment of equal wages to Inter-state migrant workmen doing same type of work in the establishment alongwith local labourers. In any case the payment of wages fixed under the minimum wages Act 1948 for that kind of work.

iv) Payment of displacement allowance which is equivalent to 50% of monthly wages payable to the Inter-state migrant workmen. It shall not be refundable and shall be in addition to the wages on other dues payable to him.

v) The journey allowance of sum not less than the fair from the place of residence of the workmen in his state in the place of work in other state besides payment of wages during the period of his Journey as if he is on duty.

vi) Suitable residential accommodation facilities to the workman.

vii) Prescribed medical facilities to the workman including free charge of hospitalization.

viii) Protective clothing to the workman in cold climate.

ix) Submission of report to the specified authorities of both the states and also news to the kinds of workmen in case of fatal accident or serious bodily injuries to the workman.

The above provisions as embodied in the law are required to be compiled with by the contractors recruiting Inter-state migrant workmen. In the event of failure to implement the provisions of the Act by the Contractor, the principal employer is required to implement the provisions.

Extent of Operation

The Act applies, inter alia:

i) To every establishment in which five or more inter-state migrant workmen or employed.

ii) To every contractor who employs or who employed five or more Inter-State migrant worker on any day of the proceeding twelve months.

The Act extends to the whole of India. It applies to establishments and to the contractors as defined in see (21-b) of the Act where in five or more workmen are employed on any day of the proceeding twelve months as Inter-state migrant workmen.

Establishment (Section 62 (1-D) of the Act):

The term establishment means any office or Department of the Government or a local authority or any place where any industry, trade, business, manufacture or occupation carried on.

Principal Employer (See-24) (G) of the Act

Under this enactment the Principal employer means :

i) In relation to any office or department of the Government or a local authority or such other officer as the Government or the case may be, may specify in this behalf.

ii) In relation to a factory the owner or occupier of the factory and where a person has been named as the manager of the factory under the factories Act, 1948, the person so named.

iii) In relation to any other establishment, any person responsible or the supervision and control of the establishment.

Workmen (Section 2 (i) (i–3) of the Act)

The definition of workmen is the adoption of the definition of the workman given in the Industrial Dispute Act 1947. It include :

i) any person employed in connection with the work of an establishment.

ii) to do skilled, semi-skilled, un-skilled, manual, supervisory, technical or clerical work.

iii) for hire or reward and the term of employment be expressed or implied. It does not include any such person:

a) Who is employed mainly in managerial or administrative capacity or

b) Who being employed in a supervisor capacity, draws wages exceeding 1600 rupees per medium or exercises either by the nature of the duties attached to the officer or by reason of the powers vested in him, factions mainly of a managerial nature.

Contractor

The term "Contractor" in relation to an establishment has been defined under section 2 (i) (b) as person who undertakes as an independent contractor/agent/employee or otherwise to produce a given result for the establishment. The definition of "Contractor" includes Sub-Contractor, Khatadar, Sandar or agent or any other person by whatever name called who recruit or employs workmen.

In a judgement by the Supreme court in the matter of write petition No. 2135 of 1982 filled by Bandhana Mukti Morcha against the union of India and others, a broad connotation to the definition of Contractor was given. This case related to stone queries in Faridabad area. In that judgement it was held that if there is any agreement or understanding between the Jamadar, Thikadar on the one hand and the owner of the stone Crushers on the other, that the Jamadar or Inikadar will ensure a certain rate of output of stone to be fed to the stone crusher the Jamadar or the Thikadar would be the 'contractor'.

Definition of Inter-State Migrant Workmen

Section 2 (i) (e) of the Act defines an "Inter-state migrant workman as:

i) Any person who is recruited by or through a contractor in one state.

ii) Under an agreement or other arrangement.

iii) For employment in and establishment in another state whether with or without the knowledge of the principal employer in relation to such establishment,

To satisfy this definition, three main conditions are to be fulfilled i.e.

a) the reason should be recruited by a 'Contractor' in one state.

b) The mode of recruitment may be through an agreement or any other arrangement

c) the recruitment should be for employment in state other than where such recruitment was done.

The word 'recruitment' has been defined under the Act under section

2 (i) (b) as entering into an agreement or other arrangement for recruitment. Recruitment as per Inter-state migrant Act means any agreement whether written, oral, expressed or implied.

The Honourable Supreme court in its decision in writ petition No. 2735 of 1982 held that if the old had brings persons from their respective states at the instance of the contractors that will also be a mode of recruitment under this Act and the workman so brought will be inter-state migrant workman.

The Bonded Labour System (Abolition) Act, is implicable to the Inter-state migrant workmen, because in most of the cases the advance paid to the Inter-state migrant workmen before they are brought for work is treated as debt/loan given to the migrant workmen. In most of the cases, they are paid less than the minimum wages. There was a bill introduced in the Rajya Sabha to amend the Act by way of incorporating on to a person who had initially contact labour/migrant labour would be treated as bond labour for the purpose of release and rehabilitation if it fulfills the criteria of bonded labour system defined in the Act. This is initiated in order to attract the attention of the Enforcement authorities that benefits under Bonded Labour System (Abolition) Act 1976 could be extended to Inter state migrant workers/contract labour also.

The definition of "Inter-State Migrant Workmen" as given in Section 2 (i) (e) of the Act may create a doubt whether it will apply also to such of the employees of any recruitment made in an all India basis or State wise for employment in its regular establishment and happen to work in a state other than the state where they have been recruited. To avoid any likelihood of any mischief in the recruitment of persons from one state for employment in another state an exemption clause has been included in this Act in the form of Section 31. This section gives the appropriate Govt., the power to exempt in special cases by way of notification in the official gazette subject to such conditions and restrictions if any and for such specified period or periods from all or any provisions of the Act and Rules.

Registration of Establishment of Principal Employers

Similar to the Scheme of contract labour (R & A) Act, 1979 a regulatory provision has been made in this Act also, by way of putting an obligation on the part of the principal employer in whose establishment Inter-State Migrant Workmen are employed to get his establishment registered with the respective authorities depending on whether establishment is in the Central sphere of State sphere.

Registering Officer

Section 3 of the Act empowers the State Govt. for appointment of Registering Officer. Accordingly the Assistant Labour Commissioner, Dadan Cell and the Deputy Labour Commissioner, Cuttack/Sambalpur/ Jeypore and Rourkela have been appointed as Registering Officer in the State of Orissa.

Section 4 (i) read with rule 3 requires the principal employer to apply for registration in the prescribed form delivered personally or by Registered post accompanied with treasury Challan showing deposit of required fee and the registering officer shall acknowledge the receipt of such application after noting the data of receipt on the application. Section 4 (2) and Section 4 (3) and rule 4 of the Act set the time limit for the Registering Officer within which he has to issue registration certificate in the prescribed form. Section 4(2) read with Rule 5 empowers the Registering Officer to reject incomplete applications. The Registering Officer can also effect an amendment on receipt of intimation under Rule 4(3) that change has occurred in the particulars specified in the certificate of registration.

Revocation of Registration : Section 5 authorises the Registration Officer to revoke the registration Certificate if he is satisfied that the registration has been obtained by misrepresentation or suppression of material fact or for any other reason, after giving the principal employer an opportunity of being hear and after obtaining prior approval of the appropriate Govt. The order should be in writing and communicated to the principal employer.

Effect of non-registration : Section 5 of the Act prohibits the principal employer to employ Inter State Migrant Workmen without obtaining a certificate of registration.

Licensing of Contractor

Section 7 of the Act empowers the appropriate Government as licensing Officer. Accordingly the State Govt. has appointed the Deputy Labour Commissioner, Cuttack, Sambalpur, Jaypore and Rourkela and the Assistant Labour Commissioner, Dadan Cell as the Licensing officer under the Act in respect of their respective jurisdictions.

Section 8 prohibits employment of Inter State Migrant workmen in an establishment except under or in accordance with a licence issued by the Licensing Officer.

That apart specific provision has been made under clause 9 (2) of Orissa Rules that the local agents who supply migrant workmen to the contractors of the outside State or work either as a sub-contractor or a commission agent of such contractor shall have to obtain a licence from the concerned licensing officer of the state from which migrant workmen are recruited and drafted to outside State on making an equivalent as provided under Rule 13(2).

Licensing Procedure

Section 9 read with Rule 7 prescribes procedure for making application by the contractor and grant of license by the Licensing Officer. It provides that the contractor is required to submit (i) application in the prescribed form in duplicate (ii) certificate of the principal employers in the prescribed form (iii) the required to note the date of receipt of application on the body of the application itself and grant acknowledgment for granting or refusing licence. The Licensing Officer is authorized to take into account matters prescribed under Rule 8. If the licensing is of the opinion that licence must not be granted he should afford reason all opportunity to the applicant to be, heard. There after, he must convey his decision of rejecting the application by written order given reasons or such refusal (Rule-10). The term and conditions of the licence are prescribed under rule 11. The licence is not transferable and shall be valid or a period of one year which can be renewed after expiry of the period i.e. 31st December of the year in which the licence has been issued. The procedure and period of renewal of license are prescribed under Rule 14 and 15.

Revocation, Suspension and Amendment of Licence

Under Section the Licensing Officer on being satisfied can revoke licence and forfeit the Security furnished by the Contractor, if (i) the licence has been obtained by misrepresentation or suppression of material facts (ii) there has been either non-compliance (without a reasonable cause) or contravention of any of the conditions of the licence. The order of the revocation shall be made after the holder of the licence has been given reasonable opportunity of being heard. The licensing officer is also authorized to suspend the operation of the licence, pending such revocation one, or forfeiture of security as imposed does not effect the liability of the holder of the licence to any other penalty. The licensing officer is authorized to affect an amendment on application of the licence holder alongwith deposit of the prescribed fees by him. In case the Licensing Officer refuses to make the amendment sought, the reasons shall be recorded in writing and conveyed to the applicant. The Registering Officer. Licensing Officer are exercising quasi/judicial functions under the Act. They should give due attention to the details and ensure proper recording of the order following the principle of nature justice.

Security Deposit and Fees

The State Govt, by virtue of notification has specified the security deposit under the sub-section (3) of Section 8. rule 10,17 provides for the procedure regarding adjustment and refund of the Security deposits. The security amount may be refunded to licence holder on satisfaction of the licensing officer that there is no breach of conditions of licence and there is no order for the forfeiture of security. If the licence holder does not want the security deposits to be adjusted in respect of his fresh application or does not intend to get licence renewed then he has to make an application in the prescribed arm to the licensing officer. The fees to be paid for grand of license under Section 7 is prescribed under rule 12.

Appeals and Procedure

Section 11 Provides a right of appeal to the person aggrieved by an older made under section 4,5,8 and section 10. Any appeal preferred against the order or registering licensing officer shall satisfy following points :

i) It shall be made with 30 days of the date of communication of the order.

ii) It shall be accompanied by required Treasury Challan of Rs. 25.

iii) It should be signed by the applicant or his authorized agent and

iv) The ground of appeal shall be distinctly and precisely mentioned for every decision of rejecting, accepting, restoring, modifying, varying, the appellate officer shall record reasons. The Labour Commissioner, Orissa, Dy. Labour Commissioners and the Asst. Labour Commissioner, Dadan cell have been appointed as specified Authority for the purpose of section 12 and 16 of the Act.

Responsibility Towards Payment of Wages

Section 17 of the Act read with Rules 25 to 35 makes the contractor responsible for payment of wages to the workers employed by him and lays down the procedure to be followed, Section 17 (4) makes it obligatory on the part of the principal employer to pay the wages in case the contractor fails to do so. The principal employer is authorised to recover the amount from the contractor by way of deduction from the amount due to the workers from the contractor's bill.

Responsibility Towards Payments of Allowances

Section 14 and 15 of the Act provides an obligation on the contractor to pay every Inter State Migrant Workmen displacement allowance and journey allowance in addition to the wages payble to him. The period of journey will be included in the period and wages of this period shall be payble by the contractor. Section 18 read with rule 16 days down that any allowance payble by the contractor shall be paid by the principal employer on the former's failure to do so.

Welfare and Other Facilities

Section 16 read with rules 36 to 45 makes it obligatory on the part of the contractor to provide free medical facilities, protective clothing, drinking water, latrine, urinals, washing facilities, rest rooms canteens, and residential accomodation. If the contractor fails to do so, it shall be provided by the principal employer.

Rate of Wages

Section 13 read with Rule 25 to 33 requires the contractor to pay the inter State Migrant Workmen Wages in no case less than the rates fixed under the Minimum Wages Act 1948. If they are engaged in work which are same or similar to the work performed by other workmen in the establishment the rate of wages shall be the same shall in no case be less than those paid by the principal employer to a workman of lowest category directly employed by him in that establishment. The payment shall be made in cash in presence of authorized representative of the principal employer and shall be made on any working day at the work premises during working hours on a date notified in advance.

Register, Records And Notices

Section 22 read with Rules 48 & 49 every principal employer shall maintain (i) Register of contractor (ii) Register of persons employed as Inter State Migrant workmen. Annual Return in form XXIV shall be submitted to the Registering Officers under Rule 56. Registers/ returns to be maintained and submitted by the Contractor are :

i) Register of persons employed

ii) Displacement-Cum-outward journey allowance sheet and return journey allowances register.

iii) Master Roll

iv) Register of Wages

v) Register of fines

vi) Register of deductions,

vii) Register of advances

viii) Register of overtime

ix) Half yearly return to the licensing officer.

All registers and records maintained by the principal employer/ contractor shall be preserved for 3 calender year and shall be kept in an officer or building in the precincts of the work place of the place specified by the Inspector. Under Rules 55, the notice to be displayed by the contractor/ principal employer are (i) Notices of rate of wages (ii) Notice of items of work (iii) Notice of wage period (iv) Notice of dates of payment of wages (v) Notices of name an address of the Inspector.

Legal Action

Section 28 of the Act read with rule 60 (2) of the Orissa rules provides that all offences are timbale by Court of 1st judicial magistrate Metropolitan Magistrate on a complaint made by the previous sanction in writing by the chief Inspector. Section 25 provides that whoever contravenes by provision of this act or of any rules made there under shall be punishable with fine which may extend up to one thousand rupees or with imprisonment or a term which may extend to one year or with both. For continuing offense an additional fine which may extend to one year or with both. For continuing offense an additional fine which may extend upto Rs. 100 for each day of the period for which such contravention continues after conviction for first such contravention.

Inspecting Staff

Section 20 of the Act employers the State Govt. to appoint such persons as it thinks fit to be Inspectors for the purpose of this act by notification in official Gazette defining the local limits within which they shall exercise their powers. The State Govt. has appointed the Labour Commissioner, Deputy Labour Commissioner, Assistant Labour Officers and the Rural Labour Inspectors as Inspectors under the Act.

The Primary duty of the Inspector as denied under Section 20 of the Act is to identify the establishments where Inter State Migrant workmen are employed and they should take steps for getting the establishment of the Principal employer covered by the act, registered and the establishment of the contractor covered by the Act duly licensed.

Inspectors have been empowered with the powers of entry, examination, search and seizure and other powers to enforce the Act. The inspectors have also powers to call for any information or statistics in relation to migrant workmen from any contractor or principal employer at any time order in writing and such contractor and the principal employer are legally bound to do so (Rule 57).

The technique of Inspections to be carried out under the Act and the Rules will be more or less the same as under Contract Labour (Regulation and Abolition) Act, 1970 and rules made thereunder.

Section 24 of the Act provides for punishment for the person who obstructs an Inspector in discharge of his duties under this Act or willfully neglects to afford the inspector or the authorised person any reasonable facility for making any inspect on, examination, inquiry or investigation etc. The punishment may extend to two years of imprisonment or with fines which may extend to two years of imprisonment or with fines which may extend to Rs. 2,000/- or with both.

Miscellaneous Provisions

Section 21 of the Act provides schedule specifying six enactments namely :-

1) The Workmen's Compensation Act, 1923.

2) The Payment of Wages Act, 1936.

3) The Industrial Disputes Act, 1947.

4) The Employees State Insurance Act, 1948.

5) The Employees Provident Fund and Miscellaneous Provisions Act, 1952.

6) The Maternity Benefit Act, 1961.

For the purpose of enactments the Inter-State Migrant Workmen shall on and from the date of his recruitment to be employed and actually worked in the establishment or as the case may be, the first establishment in connection with work in which he is employed.

Under Section 19, it is the duty of every contractor and every principal employer to ensure that any loan given by such contractor of principal employer to any Inter state Migrant Workmen does not remain outstanding after the completion of the period of employment under the said contractor or Principal employer. The Obligation of Inter State Migrant workmen to repay any debt obtained from the contractor or principal employer and remaining unsatisfied before the completion of such employment be deemed to have been extinguished on completion of the employment. Also no suit or other proceedings shall be in any court or before any authority for the recovery of such debt or any part thereof.

Under Section 22 all disputes relating to employment, non-employment or terms of employment or condition of labour can be taken up by authorities of the home state of workmen if they have returned after completion of employment and before the expiry of six months at the instance of the workmen. Transfer of proceedings from State to another State is legal and the Central Govt. as the case may be is the appropriate authority on this score.

Section 30 gives an ever riding effect over any other law, agreement or contract of service etc. Which are inconsistent with the provisions of this Act. However, if under any other law, agreement or contract of source the Inter State Migrant Workmen are getting more favourable benefits, then these benefits shall continue and the Inter State Migrant Workmen will continue to get other benefits also from this Act.

After the commencement of the Central Act the State Government have appointed Registering Officer, Licensing Officer, Specified Authority, Chief Inspector and Inspector for the purpose of enforcement of provisions of the said Act.

After enforcement of the Central Act in this State all the Dadan Labour Agents were advised to apply for the licence as per the new Act. The G.R.P. have been requested to co-operate with the field officers for taking action in the matter of unauthorized recruitment. Due publicity was made through local news papers and A.I.R. to arouse awareness among all concerned about the rights and responsibilities of migrant workmen and the contractors. The Inspectors are conducting regular inspections and surprise checks to detect unauthorised recruitment and to ensure compliance of other requirements of law, as a result of which a large number of unauthorized recruitment have been detected and prosecutions filled against the defaulting agents and contractors. Seminars and meetings including training camps are being conducted regularly at different village pockets of migrant prone areas to educate the public about the provisions of the Inter-State Migrant Workmen (RE & CS) Act, 1979. Whenever complaints are received about different types of harassment, immediate steps are being taken. The concerned Labour Commissioners are moved to render necessary assistance for arranging discreet inquires as well as to rescue the concerned migrant workmen with realisation of their legal dues and way expenses. Besides some officers of the Labour Directorate are also deputed to different work sites to arrange rescue of workers with payment of their legal dues and way expenses.

In addition to the above, one Assistant Labour Commissioner was posted at New Delhi to look after the problems of migrant workmen in the Northern States like Jammu & Kashmir, Himachal Pradesh, Delhi, Punjab and Haryana. He was also being advised to look into the problems of the migrant workers working in other State as and when such contingency arises.

Legislative Measures

There was no effective machinery to save the poor Dadan Labourers from the exploitative clutches of the avaricious contractors. Thus, the agony of these Dadan Labourers under the wheel of ruthless exploitation made by contractors increased in gigantic magnitude. It was only in 1975 that the State Legislative Assembly in a bid to extirpate such pernicious practices enacted an act called "The Orissa Dadan Labour (Control and Regulation) Act, 1975 which was enforced from 1st January 1976. Alongwith it various other measures under payment of wages act, Minimum Wages Act, Contract Labour (Regulation and Abolition) Act and Workmen's Compensation Act were implemented in Order to regulate the terms and conditions of recruitments of Dadan Labour registration of agents etc. But these remedial measures proved insufficient to protect the workers from the whims and caprices of the Contractors. Therefore, in order to diametrically annihilate such amounting tendencies, the Government has recently taken a more concrete step by another enactment known as Inter-State Migrant Workmen (Regulation of employment and condition of services) Act 1979 which was given effect from 27th Sept. 1980. The present Act mainly deals with the registration of contractors, and their duties, determination of the rate of wage and its method of payment all sort of medical facilities, legal aids, condition of work and other welfare aspects like canteen, rest-rooms, protective clothing, residential accommodations etc. It also clearly prescribes power and duties of the authorities under the Act and penalties to be imposed upon the contractors if rules are violated by them.

A Policy Thrust

Migration either with the state or inter-state, effect the distribution or resources—especially, human capital. The economic and social effect of migration are important to the development of both the place of origin and those of destination. The direction of flow from rural to urban area, affects the regional development of the place of migrants origin and contributes to the problem of urban growth.

The rural development of Orissa get a continuous set back due to labour out-migration as the state is deprived of its work force which if absorbed inside the state will uplift the economy from poverty and stagnation.

It is seen that attempts to stem the tide of labour migration in Orissa have not been successful. What does seem apparent is that unless the socio-economic circumstances of the sending and receiving areas alter radically, the labour migration in Orissa will continue, spelling disaster and despair to the economy.

The urgent need of the hour is heavy investment in the traditional sector as well as in industrially backward region for adequate employment creation. Since modern manufacturing industries are expected to absorb only a limited number of labourers, adequate employment can be created in small- scale industries, construction works, labour-intensive road works afforestation, animal husbandry, fishery and the like.

With regard to Dadan labour, it may be well said the problem can be solved if they themselves become conscious of their rights. They must get united without reserving personal motives and unitedly fight for the fulfillment of their basic needs in consistent with the labour they are being harassed by the contractors and Khatadars, they should immediately bring the instance to the notice of the concerned authority under the Government of Orissa. The success of the Legislative measures lies in its strict and proper implementation. The Officers employed to carry out the provisions of the Act must be sincere and honest in performing of their duties. They must be sympathetic enough towards the sorrowful causes of the exploited labourers. In reality, it is observed that many contractors without registering their names are proceeding on their business and economically butchering workers by not paying them their due. Hence, the Government should catch out and reprimand them with drastic punishment so that it may be a lesson for all others of the same category not to resort to these practices. The press should also pay a vital role in ameliorating the lots of the dying labourers by publishing cases of harassment inflicted by the contractors upon the workers.

3

Theoretical Perspectives on Migration and Methodological Design

This Chapter outlines briefly the theoretical perspectives on migration to ascertain the determinants of migration. Besides, the study focuses on the samples technique and methodology adopted for field exploration.

Process of Migration

Seen in the wide sweep of history, labour migration has been an integral and vital part of human development. Infact, the history of population migration is as old as man itself.

Labour migration may be defined as a form of labour mobility towards districts or states or out-side where industry and employment are expanding. In other-words, migration may be the phenomenon of the flow of people over shorter or longer distances from one origin to a destination either for temporary or permanent settlement.

Some social scientists have analysed migration in terms of psychological differences between movers and non-movers. Some have attempted to illustrate movements in terms of individual migrant's revealed 'reasons'. Some have highlighted on socio-economic structural characteristics of different areas, and others have discussed on geographical or natural resource factors.

Infact, conceptualising territorial mobility is a complex process. Because it includes four crucial dimensions—space, residence, time and activity changes.

The notion of migration as has been referred earlier, implies a movement from one place to another. The place or area constitutes on important aspect of migration. Areas that may be similar or distinguishable on the basis of economic parameters like levels of income, structure of production etc. may not be identical on the basis of demographic, cultural or political considerations.

The concept of distance plays a vital role in understanding the process of migration. There are three important elements associated with the concept of 'distance'. They are—geographical, economic and social.

Geographical approaches to migration stipulate to movement of people over log distances where-as short-distance movements are regarded as 'residence' change. Thus, inter-state movements are termed as migration, Hence, migration of rural people of Orissa to Surat in our analysis serves the purpose of out-migration. Intra-rural migration is heavily dominated by women in our country mainly due to local moves for marriage.

With regard to economic distance, we understand such movements which are undertaken between market centres or between centres of production or centres of particular types of industry, or occupational specialisation. However, a concept of economic distance should be founded upon costs and availability of communication, information and transport networks.

Social distance could be used to categorise the types of move in terms of physical, separation from an accustomed circle of family and neighbours, and from a particular ethnic group or social group.

Migration may be classified on the basis of 'duration of stay' Labourers may move 'permanently' or for a prolonged period. They may move for a short-period.

The labourers can be termed as 'migratory labourers' most suitably to the permanent migrants.

The circular migrants are known as 'turnover migrants' or 'pendular migrants' or 'largest migrants' or 'short term' migrants. Under such migration process, a move is made for a short period with the intention of returning to a peace of usual residence.

An important group of circular migrants consists of 'seasonal migrants', those who combine activities in several places according to seasonal labour requirements and availability of seasonal work opportunities.

Those who change activity by not usual residence consists of life-cycle stage migrants. In many pre-industrial societies youths leave their home village on approaching adulthood in order to gain experience and to ensure their social status in the village after they return. Step-migrants are those do not have the intention of returning to their area of origin, at least not in the foreseeable future. Step migrants are those who have been defined as moving from a rural area to small urban area and then to a larger urban area and ultimately a city, making in effect two or more, moves before they settle in their long-term, destination.

Non-migrants may be termed as those who have never moved or who have not moved either area of residence or activity within a specified period.

Potential migrants could be identified as those wishing to move, if the circumstances allowed or the opportunities arose.

Active migrants are those who act as pioneer movers, and whose locational behaviours are not co-ordinated with that or other migrants.

A passive migrant is one "in selecting a destination is dependent on earlier migrants."

"The active migrant is distinguished by his pioneering characteristics. This pioneering can be absolute, that is, he can be the first settler in uninhabited territory, but more likely it is relative. The active migrant may be considered as the source of the voluntary chain migration process which frequently, but not always, ensues."

Many people move in order to alter a life-style or change economic or social status. These have been classified as innovative migrants.

On the contrary, others move in order to retain a life-style or status or to re-obtain what they have lost. And therefore, it can be defined as 'defensive or conservative migrants.'

With explicit focus on landholding of the migrant labourers, a distinction can be made between reversible migrants and non-reversible migrants.

Reversible migrants were defined as those who own land in the village, even though they may own land elsewhere as well. They leave village to make up a deficit or to earn extra income, and their options are:

i) Return to village

ii) Reside elsewhere

iii) Shuttle between the new area and their village or origin.

On the contrary, non-reversible migrants own no village land and have little option other than to reside elsewhere.

Incidence of Migration

It is interesting to draw a distinction between a rate of migration and the incidence of migration. A rate of migration refers to the ratio of the number of migrants to the total population, where the moves have occurred in a specific period. Determinants of a rate of migration from one area to another may be quite different from those factors that determine the incidence of migration.

The incidence of migration refer to the differential rate of migration across identifiable demographic or social groups. In this context, migratability should be separated from migrant status. A group may be more migratable than other, depending upon their relative attachment to the area, but whether or not migration will take place depend on socio-economic influences.

Generally, wage labourers are more migratable. But their movements are influenced by relative incomes in various areas, degree of effective coercion, fluctuations in general living conditions or changes in relative livings conditions.

Gross and Net-migration

Gross in migration or gross out-migration refers to the number of people who enter or leave an area in a given period. The sum of in-migrants and out-migrant is the population turnover, expressed as a rate it divided by the population at risk at the beginning or end of the period.

Net in-migration or net out migration is the balance after out migrants or in-migrants respectively have been deducted from the gross glow.

$$\text{Inflow rate} = \frac{\text{Number of in - migrants in area}}{\text{Population in area at beginning of period}}$$

$$\text{In- migration rate} = \frac{\text{Number of in - migrants}}{\text{Population in area at end of period}}$$

In the absence of actual migration data, some indirect methods of calculating net migration are adopted.

Net in-migration = Population growth — Natural increase.

Migration may be group migration or mass migration.

Group migration occurs when all or a large proportion of an identifiable group migrate at about the same time and in the same direction, usually for similar purposes.

Mass migration occurs when whole communities participate in migration process, which becomes a social pattern of behaviour. In our analysis, the brick-kiln labourers of drought prone tribal belong to the category of mass migration.

Chain Migration

Chain-like movements have been taken to describe situations in which an individual and family migration in longitudinal perspective.

Chain migration can be defined as that movement in which prospective migrants learn of opportunities, and one provided with transportation and employment arranged by means of primary social relationship with previous migrants.

Ravenstein in his famous 'Laws of Migration' (1885) have analysed 'stage migration' and 'step migration.'

Step migration refers to the process of successive moves by one migrant. Stage migration refers to a social pattern, a process by which some groups move from the countryside to villages or small towns. Some other people move from small towns to large towns and some others from towns to large cities.

Migratory Moments:

While illustrating various concepts that have featured in research on migration, it is not worthy to focus on migratory moments.

Migration process in terms of a series of behavioural phases are termed as migration moments.

Conceptualising the mobility process as a series of key moments should help in the refinement of explanatory models. The possible migratory moments are as follows:

i) Migration not even considered,

ii) Migration considered but rejected:

—for indefinite future, or

—temporarily, on a contingency basis,

iii) Migration intended/planned, but timing and/or destination uncertain,

iv) Migration in process,

v) Migration completed,

vi) Migration made, returned to area of origin or place of previous residence.

The complexity of the demographic phenomenon of population mobility and its multiple dimensions have been briefly out-lined in the proceeding paragraphs.

Reasons of Migration

Dislike of agricultural work, 'to obtain cash' and worsening of economic situation were the most frequently cited reasons for migration.[1]

Family considerations play an important role in migration. The underlying objective of migration is maximization of benefits of the entire family, rather than of purely individual benefits.[2]

The causes of motivations for migration of the rural poor to Surat town as ascertained from the interview schedules are manifold the common ones are:

i) Expanding employment opportunities in the growing Surat town in contrast to the income constraints in villages.

ii) Encouragement or inducement by friends and relatives in Surat

iii) The social injustice faced by the rural community in the villages.

iv) The high hopes and dreams of an assured means of employment and thereby, a better life in any critical situation etc.

v) In India, females are found in large number in short-distances migration (marriage migration) while for long distances migration males are pre-dominant. From 1961 and 1971 census it was revealed that males migrated twice as much as the females. However, female migration is basically associated with marriage.

Kalahandi, the poverty ridden district which has been hitting the headlines for its starvation deaths and sale of babies, is also reported to have the highest number of child marriages. It is found that those who married early had to face early parenthood, unplanned and unwanted pregnancies, deprivation of educational opportunities, low-paying jobs and limited choices for the future. In some instances, some mothers were forced into prostitution for their living.'

Earlier studies made by Dr. Tripathy[3] confirms the fact that because of drought situation and object poverty the problem of bonded labour, sale of child, child labour and mass migration of labour to near by states of Andhra Pradesh and Madhya Pradesh has existent. It has posed a challenging and herculean problem to halt the process of mass migration of tribal labourers of Kalahandi.

However, most studies reveal that the vital streams of labour migration are rural-rural, rural-urban, urban-urban and urban-rural.

To repeat, since the principal current of modern migration analysis all over the World is towards urban areas, the present work attempts to examine the problems of rural out-migration in Orissa.

Theoretical Perception on Migration

Theoretical illustrations of rural-urban migration have a long history, dating from atleast the 1880's when Revenstein presented his 'Laws of Migration'. According to this law, migrants move from areas of low opportunity to areas of high opportunity. The choice of destination of regulated by distance, with migrants tending to move to nearby places.

Revenstein's laws of migration restated by Everett Lee in 1956, To him, the forces exerting an influence on migrant perceptions into 'Push' and 'Pull' factors. The former are 'negative' factors which force migrants to leave origin areas, while the latter are 'positive' factors attracting migrants to destination areas.

The Lewis-fie-Ranis model was formulated in 1954 by Prof. W. A. Lewis, later extended by Prof. Gustav Ranis and John Fei (1961). This modern recognizes migration as an equi-liberating mechanism which, through transfer of labour from the labour surplus to the deficit sector, leading to wage equality in the two sectors. This model assumes a dual economy, consisting of two sectors (*i*) traditional agricultural sector with zero or very low productivity surplus labour and (*ii*) a high productivity modern urban industrial sector which absorbs labour from the subsistence sector through gradual transfer.

In 1962, Sjaastad advanced a theory of migration which considers the decision to migrate as an investment decision involving an individual expected costs and returns over time.

In the body of economic literature known as the Haris Todaro (J.R. Harris and M.P. Todaro 1970) model explores that the decision to migrate from rural to urban centres is fundamentally related to two principal variables (i) Urban-rural real income differentials, and (ii) the probability of obtaining a job in an urban area.

The influx of new migrants add themselves to a pool of unemployed or underemployed urban residents what consequently turns off the flow of migrants to the urban is that the 'expected' urban income for any new migrant drops. The flow of migrants is absolutely stopped when the 'expected' urban income equals the expected rural income.

Methodology of the Study

The methodology of the study depend on both primary and secondary sources of data. The report of the labour commission of Orissa conducted a study on inter-state migrant labourers from Orissa which pointed out largest number of migrants belong from the district of Ganjam. However, the causes and consequences of such migrants have not been satisfactorily explained by researchers. From the economic parlance, free migration of workers assume significance as it can bring adjustments (in both quality and quantity) between the supply of and demand for regional labour, especially in the short run. In a developing country like ours, the main thrust of policy implication is bring about the full employment of labour resources in long run. Since a knowledge of determinants of the market adjustments of inter-regional (or inter-state) labour supply through worker migration depend on various factors of socio-economic importance, it is imperative to study the reasons of migration of one household in comparison with the non-migrants households of the same village and socio-economic impact on migrant households.

Ganjam district covered an area of 12,5365 square Kilometers, out of 4,698 villages, 4265 villages are inhabited and 433 villages are uninhabited, divided into 14 tahasils. There are 466 Gram Panchayats under 29 Blocks and 4 sub-divisions. In Urban set-up, there are two municipalities and 18 notified area councils in the district.

According to 1991 census there are 31,42,120 population in the district out of which, 26,02,714 (82.81%) population residing in villages. The scheduled caste and scheduled tribe population constitute about 12.76 percent and 8.05 percent respectively of the total population. Density of population per square kilometer is 251 as per 1991 census in the district.

Agriculture is the main thrust of the economy. Out of the total main workers, there are 39 thousand (42. 13%) cultivators and 30 thousand (32.46%) agricultural labourers who depend on it.

Since the district of Ganjam ranks first in the list of having largest number of migrants from Orissa,* it is the primary reason of selecting the district for the study of rural out-migration to other states. (See Annexure–I)

---

* Report of the labour Commissioner, Orissa Bhubaneswar. Inter-state migrant workmen in Orissa: A study (Ganjam and Puri district) 1989.

Out of total 29 blocks two blocks selected randomly and list of villages collected from both block offices. For selection of villages, simple random sampling method is used. Then from among the villages households were listed to identify migrant and non-migrant households. (See Annexure–II)

The data were collected through personal interview method with the help of a structured questionnaire after pre-testing. In order to make a comparative analysis of socio-economic position of migrant households, we have taken approximately an equal number of non-migrant households of similar economic condition from the villages surveyed.

Selection of the Field

Keeping in view the constraints of time and cost, it was decided to collect data for this enquiry from eight villages only 4 of them from Aska and rest 4 from Digapahandi block of Ganjam district. These two blocks are migrant prone blocks and migrants of the villages belonging to these blocks have been contacted earlier, these blocks are selected by using the method of simple Random sampling (SRS) for the study. Due to coincidence of the fact that these two blocks are not only the native places of the researchers but also their working places for the last 10 years.

To identify migrant households, all villages have been surveyed. The households which is having atleast one migrant workmen working for period of not less than 6 months in a year by the time of survey has been treated as a migrant household for this study. However, while selecting non-migrant households, care has been taken not to include such households who had migrated during the last two years.

Selection of Families

As has been explained earlier at first, all the household of the villages were enlisted in order to short out migrant and non-migrant households. Secondly, from among the non-migrant households, we selected a list of households who had not migrated earlier during last two years. Thus, for the purpose of the present study a total of 268 migrant households and 266 non-migrant households and 266 non-migrant households have been surveyed.

Data Through Observation Method

In addition to the filled in questionnaire, observations relevant to the study were recorded in the form of field notes. Due to our close association with these migrant villages, this method became fruitful for this study.

In addition to the primary sources of data collected through the methods analysed above, secondary source of data were accumulated from various government reports, journals, books, news papers to supplements the study.

Period of Study

The study has been conducted during March '93 April '94 at different intervals, keeping in view the convenience of the migrant households and the family members present in the village, interviews were conducted. We had to keep contact regarding the return or movement of migrant households for collection of data. However, the problem of collection of information or data with regard to non-migrant households in not so difficult as they were contacted in the agricultural field or in their households during their leisure time.

Mostly, the migrant households were contacted during panasankranti, and during Durgapuja vacation. Infact, the epidemic like plague broke-out at Surat compelled all most all the migrants to return to their villages, which facilitated to hold interviews during their presence in the villages.

As has been said earlier, in view of the financial implications in such studies, and other busy schedules, of researchers and academic work, the researchers could not survey more villages.

However, all endeavours have been taken to make the study just, appropriate and genuine so as to generalize the findings for the district as well as the state. It is hoped, that the study will immensely benefit the planners, policy-makers, demographers, social-scientists, labour administrators and researchers to formulate policy measures.

The Table 3.1 presents the list of villages surveyed, the number of migrant households as well as the number of non-migrant households surveyed in each village. It is found that Malati village of Aska block has the highest percentage of migrant households while Khamarigam of Digapahandi block has the lowest percentage of migrant households. This may be due to the availability of irrigation facilities by Ghodahada dam in Khamarigam.

Table 3.1 : Number of Migrants and Non-migrants Households Surveyed from the List of Villages

Sl. No.	*Village*	*Migrant Households*	*Non-Migrant Households*	*Total Households*
1.	Baritola	09 (12.5)	09 (12.5)	72
2.	Bijoy Padmanavpur–Ladigam	31 (15.0)	31 (15.0)	207
3.	Khamarigam	09 (5.7)	09 (5.7)	158
4.	Onangpur	49 (30.8)	49 (30.8)	159
5.	Khukundia–Bangarada	42 (28.0)	42 (28.0)	150
6.	Mangalpur	62 (9.0)	62 (9.0)	690
7.	Muniguda	56 (22.9)	56 (22.9)	245
8.	Malati	10 (55.6)	08 (44.4)	18
	Total	*268*	*266*	*1699*

Figures in paranthesis represent percent of migrant households to total households of the respective villages.

Limitation of Study

Undoubtedly, the study has some limitations which are as follows:

i) The migrant who were in their place of destination and not turned to their native places during the year could not be contacted.

ii) The information provided by head of the migrant households/ migrants depend on their memory as there was no written record/evidence available.

iii) The working conditions at the place of destinations of migrants could not be accurately obtained as these were not visited by the researchers.

Objective of the Study

The study has the following few objectives:

i) To assess the history of labour migration in Orissa with a view to tracing out the contributory factors for such migration.

ii) To identify the nature and types of labour migration prevalent in Orissa.

iii) To examine the socio-economic features of migrant and non-migrant households.

iv) To study the impact of migration on socio-economic conditions of rural people.

v) To make an evaluative study of Government Policy adopted to tackle the problem of labour migration.

vi) To suggest policy implications.

Scheme of the Study

As a means of achieving the afore-said objectives and to draw some meaningful confusions, the study is organized into five chapters.

Chapter-1 : History and origin of labour migration.

Chapter-2 : Problem of migrant workmen in Orissa.

Chapter-3 : Theoretical perspectives on migration and Methodological design.

Chapter-4 : Socio-Economic features of migrant and non-migrant households.

Chapter-5 : Labour out-migration and its impact.

Bibliography

References

1. Banerjee, Biswajit. "*Rural to Urban Migration and Urban Labour Market.*" Himalaya Publishing House, Bombay, 1996, p-65

2. *Ibid* p. 264,

3. Tripathy, S.N. *Bonded Labour in India*. Discovery Publishing House, New Delhi, (1989).

4. Tripathy, S.N. & Das Soudamini. *Informal Women Labour in India*. Discovery Publishing House, New Delhi (1991).

ANNEXURE — I

District-wise Representation of Dadan Labour

Name of the District from which drafted	*Approximate No. of Dadan Labourers going to other States*
Ganjam	60,000
Puri	47,000
Balasore	15,000
Mayurbhanj	10,000
Keonjhar	6,000
Phulbani	3,000
Kalahandi	3,000
Cuttack	3,000
Bolangir	1,000
Koraput	1,000
Dhenkanal	1,000
Total	**1,50,000**

Source : Labour Directorate of Orissa, Bhubaneswar.

ANNEXURE — II

Detailed Particulars of Aska and Digapahandi Block of Ganjam District

	Aska	*Digapahandi*
I. LOCATION		
1) No. of Towns	1	1
2) No. of Inhabited Villages	126	243
3) No. of Grampanchayat	21	18
4) Total Population (1981)	1,00,295	1,13,071
a) Rural Population	1,00,295	1,05,218
b) Urban Population	------	7,853
c) Population of SC/ST	13,590/743	14,143
II. OCCUPATIONAL DISTRIBUTION		
1) Cultivators (1981)	19,786	20,500

(Contd.)

ANNEXURE — II (Contd.)

Detailed Particulars of Aska and Digapahandi Block of Ganjam District

	Aska	*Digapahandi*
2) Agril. labourers and Allied Agril. Activities	569	12,538
3) Cottage Inds. & Household Industries	72	1,250
4) Other Industries	206	170
5) Trade & Commerce	1,076	1,057
6) Others	4,385	3,529
III. DISTRIBUTION OF AREAS		
1) Total reporting area	18,592	34,169.75
2) Net Cultivated Area	11,676.20	24,079.10
3) Current fallows	350	12,400
4) Area Under Forest	348.20	4,275.40
5) Area not available for cultivation	1,177.85	1,015
6) Other Cultivated Area	81.08	400
IV. IRRIGATION		
1) Net Irrigated Area in Hectares	10,367	12,770
2) % Irrigated Shown	55.76%	53.3%
V. ROPING PATTERN		
1) Double Multiple Crop Area	7.357	14,677
2) Gross Cropped Area	16.480	38,753.03
3) Area under Five Main Crops (in hec.)		
a) Paddy	11,680	15,938
b) Ragi	560	5,700
c) Groundnut	800	3,426
d) Vegetables	530	3,406
e) Others	28.20	10,283
VI. SIZE OF HOLDINGS		
1) Less than 1 Hectare	9,439	5,235
2) Between 1 & 2 Hectares	5,983	4,174

(Contd.)

ANNEXURE — II (Contd.)

Detailed Particulars of Aska and Digapahandi Block of Ganjam District

	Aska	*Digapahandi*
3) Between 2 & 4 Hectares	3,140	3,781
4) Between 4 & 10 Hectares	860	1,015
5) Between 10 & above	454	1,450
VII. BANK OFFICES		
a) State Bank Group	2	1
b) Other Public Sector Banks	4	2
c) Regional Rural Banks	4	4
d) Agril. Dev. Branches/ Gram Vikas Kendras etc.	1	---
e) Others		
1) District Central Coop. Banks	1	1
2) Land Dev. Banks	1	---
3) Urban Coop. Banks	1	---
VIII. CO-OPERATIVES		
i) No. of Primary Agril. Credit Societies (P.A.Cs) recognised	17	3
ii) No. of P.A.Cs not recognised	--	1
iii) No. of P.A.Cs having full time paid secretaries	17	4
iv) No. of Societies having own/ lived storage facilities	---	1
v) No. of Lamps	---	---
IX. OTHER INFORMATION OF OPERATIONAL SIGNIFICANCE		
1) No. of Villages with ground-water potential	164.20 Sq. KM. 1,600 Dugwells are feasible	440.32 Sq. KM 1,860 Digwells can be suck
2) Names of Villages with Veterinary Facilities	Aska (Dispensary L.I.As at Gahange Guntapada Nallabantha Ballisara and Nimina	Dispensary at Digapahandi, L.A.I at Jakar, Sidheswar Bhismagiri, Bomo-kai Talasingi, Korapada Badago-bindapur

(Contd.)

ANNEXURE — II (Contd.)

Detailed Particulars of Aska and Digapahandi Block of Ganjam District

	Aska	*Digapahandi*
3) Names of Villages having Mandi or Markets	Aska	Padmanavpur Bhismagiri Digapahandi
4) Name of Villages with concentration of rural industries	Nimina Bhatanai Podhala Hepore	Padmanavpur Bhismagiri Badagovindapur

4

Socio-Economic Features of Migrant and Non-Migrant Households

This chapter is devoted for analysing the socio-economic and demographic features of migrant as well as non-migrant households studied in terms of their age, dependence, land-holding, earnings, remittance, indebtedness, awareness etc. Some light has also been focussed to study the characteristics of the non-migrant house holds to make a comparative analysis.

In order to find out the socio-economic profile of migrant as well as non-migrant households, so as to enter some meaningful findings it is pertinent to make a field survey.

And, therefore, data on demographic information like sex, age, time of migration, reason of migration, place of origin, level of education, nature of work, awareness etc. have been collected in the survey as indicated in the methodology. This analysis may not be regarded as a definite statement of absolute magnitude, but at best indicates the general flow of persons from rural to urban region within and outside the state.

Before we analyse the field-data, it is imperative to fucus some light on the characteristic of sample village. Because, the nature of village economy, the level of development in rural areas have some influence in determining migration. Again, it is becoming increasingly clear from the recent writings on migrant workmen that source and destination areas are both likely to have attracting and repulsing elements.

Generally, migrants flow from areas where employment opportunities are stagnant, where income is low and where the rate of population growth is high. Conversely, they are attracted to area of new industrial development regions of higher per capita income and areas where the disparity between birth and death rate is less.

The Data and General Characteristics of Migrant Villages

Baritola

This village is situated 15 Kms away from Digapahandi block. The total geographical area of the village is 104.41 hectares as per revenue record. We found there are 82 households living in the village. Out of them only 9 households reported migrating their members which is 10.98 percent of the total households. The villagers are mostly depend on agricultural activities and this in turnis depend on mercy of monsoon. Failure of monsoon leads to lack of irrigation facility. The village is mainly rice growing area during Kharif Pulses and oilseed during Rabi Crop, - grown in its one-sixth of area, during which the rain is normal.

Bijepadmanavapur

It is known as ladigam in this locality and situated 5 Kms away from Digapanandi block towards east-south corner and in revenue records it is known as Bijepadmanavpur. The total geographical area of the village is 229.46 hectares. There are 231 households listed in the village and 31 households (13.42%) have reported migrant workers. This is mainly a paddy growing area. Around 3/4th of the cultivating area depend upon tank irrigation which in turn, depend upon intensity of rain.

Khamarigam

This village is located 16 Kms away from Digapahandi block. The total geographical area of the village is 204.77 hectares as per revenue records. We found there are 162 households living in the village, out of which 9 households representing 5.56 percent of total households are reported migrating their members. The inhabitants of the village are mainly engaged in agricultural activities. The Ghodahada dam irrigates most of

Table 4.1 : Total Geographical Area, Number of Households Listed and Migrant Households of Sample Villages

	Baritola	*B.P.–Ladigam*	*Khamarigam*	*Onangpur*	*K. Bangarada*	*Mangalpur*	*Munigadi*	*Malati*
1. Total Geographical Area (Hect.)	104.41	229.46	204.77	312.82	----	645.07	446.77	---
2. No. of Residential Households (As per Listing)	82	231	162	168	322	308	264	24
3. Migrant Households	9	31	9	49	42	62	56	10
4. No. of Migrant Households as percent of No. of Residential Households (listed)	10.98	13.42	5.56	29.17	13.04	20.13	21.21	41.67
5. No. of Migrants	12	35	11	53	47	66	66	10

the land and therefore, rice and other vegetables like banana, various flowers are extensively grown in this region. Indebted and poor families finding no alternative avenues of employment due to lack of land, migrate to Surat.

Onangpur

This village is located in the side of road 3 Kilometers away from the Digapahandi block towards Berhampur. The total geographical area as reported in the revenue records is 312.82 hectares. Out of 168 households living in the village 49 households representing more than 29 percent are migrant households. Though agriculture is the main occupation of the people but due to lack of irrigation most of people seek employment in informal sectors in the nearby town i.e. Berhampur. Some of them found migrating to nearby states and even to Surat for eke out a living.

K. Banagarda

This is the hamlet village of Khukundia located 17 Kilometer away from Aska Block headquarter towards north. The total geographical area of the village is 645.07 hectares with 308 residential households. Sixty-two households constituting more than 20 percent are migrant households. The migrant workmen are mostly to Surat.

Munigadi

This village is at a distance of 18 Kms. away from Aska block towards north. The total geographical area of the village is 446.77 hectares with 264 residential households as per listing. The migrant households constitute 56 which is more than 21 percent of the total households. Agricultural labourers are migrating to Madhya Pradesh, Bhubaneswar, Bihar and mostly to Surat.

Malati

The village Malati is 17 Kms away from Aska block towards North. Migrants of the village are mainly to Andhra Pradesh and Surat, who constitute more than 41 percent of the total listed households. It has been observed from the secondary sources of data presented in the Table 4.2 that both males and females migrate mostly from rural to rural during 1961 to 1981. The significant migration stream followed by rural to rural is rural to urban. In case of females the percentage increases from 9.7 to 12.5 over

Table 4.2 : Percentage Distribution of Migrants in Different Migration Streams

Sex	*Year*	*Rural to Rural*	*Rural to Urban*	*Urban to Urban*	*Urban to Rural*	*Total Migrants*
Female	1961	81.3	9.7	5.8	3.2	100.00
	1971	77.7	10.5	6.7	5.1	100.00
	1981	73.3	12.5	8.7	5.5	100.00
Male	1961	56.7	25.7	13.0	4.6	100.00
	1971	53.5	26.0	14.0	6.5	100.00
	1981	45.6	30.0	17.4	7.0	100.00

Source : Registrar General, India, New Delhi.

Note : 1) Persons born outside India were excluded.
2) 1981 Figures exclude Assam State where 1981 Census not be conducted.
3) 1961, 1971, 1981, figures are based on place of birth.

a period of 1961 to 1981. Similarly in case of males data also indicate an increasing trend as the percentage goes up from 25.7 to 30.0 during 1961 to 1981.

But one thing has to be reckoned with is the decline in the percentage of migration during 1961 to 1981 both in case of females and males form rural to rural. The secondary sources of data exhibited in Table 4.3, explain

Table 4.3 : Percentage Distribution of Migrants by Reason, 1981

	Reason of Migration	*Female*	*Male*
1.	Employment	1.9	31.8
2.	Education	1.0	5.1
3.	Family Moved	14.3	30.3
4.	Marriage	73.4	3.3
5.	Others	9.4	29.5
	Total	*100.0*	*100.0*

Source : Registrar General, India, New Delhi;
Census Monograph No. 2, 1988.
Internal Migration in India, 1961–81.

the percentage distribution of migrants by reason during 1981. It is found from the table that marriage is the important factor of migration in case of females whereas employment is the motive force of migration in case of males. The second important factor accelerating the process of migration is movement of family both in case of males and females.

Number of Migrant(s) Households

It is pertinent to note that the households having one migrant constitute 100 percent in the village Malati (Table 4.4) and more than 90 percent in three village i.e. Mangalpur (93.5%), Munigadi (92.9%) and Onangpur (91.8%) having one migrant from their households. Further, it is revealed that except Malati, all villages having households possessing two number of migrants. One-third of households of Baritola having two number of migrants. The lowest percentage of households having two number of migrants are in the village Munigadi (7.1%) followed by Mangalpur (6.5%).

Size of Household

It is found from the Table 4.5 that most of the migrant households having household size of population are 4 to 5. The percentage of households belong to this category is the highest in B. Padmanavapur (64.5 Percent) followed by village Mangalpur (61.2 Percent) except Khamarigam. It is interesting to note that migrant households of Khamarigam having population size of 6-7 is the highest (44.4%) among the villages under study. Only two villages i.e. Onangpur and Munigadi having households in the size of 10 and above are 2 and 3.5 percent respectively.

Similarly, with regard to non-migrant households, the size of households has been depicted in Table 4.6 a family size of 4–5 has been manifested in most of the non-migrant households. The percentage of households belong to this category is the highest in B. Padmanavapur (45.2) followed by both Baritola and Khamarigam (44.5 percent). It is worthwhile to mention that village Malati with household six of 1-3 holds the highest position (62.5 percent) among the non-migrant households.

Ethnic Composition of Migrant Households

Table 4.7 exhibits the caste composition of migrant households which is mainly in the category of scheduled castes and other castes

Table 4.4 : Distribution of Migrant House-holds According to Number of Migrant

Number	*Baritola*	*B.P. Ladigam*	*Khamarigam*	*Onangpur*	*Bangarada*	*Mangalpur*	*Munigadi*	*Malati*	*Total*
One	6 (66.7)	27 (87.1)	7 (77.8)	45 (91.8)	37 (88.1)	58 (93.5)	82 (92.9)	10 (100.0)	242 (82.3)
Two	3 (33.3)	4 (12.9)	2 (22.2)	4 (8.2)	5 (11.9)	4 (6.5)	4 (7.1)	---	26 × 2 52 (17.7)
Three and above	---	---	---	---	---	---	---	---	---
Total Household	9 (100.0)	31 (100.0)	9 (100.0)	49 (100.0)	42 (100.0)	62 (100.0)	56 (100.0)	10 (100.0)	268
Total Migrant	12	35	11	53	47	66	60	10	294

(Figures in the parantheses represent percent to the total)

Table 4.5 : Distribution of Migrant House-holds According to Household Size

Household Size	*Baritola*	*B.P. Ladigam*	*Khamarigam*	*Onangpur*	*Bangarada*	*Mangalpur*	*Munigadi*	*Malati*
Upto 3	2 (22.2)	4 (12.9)	2 (22.2)	1 (2.0)	5 (11.9)	3 (4.7)	10 (17.8)	1 (10.0)
4 – 5	4 (44.5)	20 (64.5)	3 (33.3)	17 (34.7)	24 (57.2)	38 (61.2)	30 (53.6)	5 (50.0)
6 – 7	2 (22.2)	3 (9.7)	4 (44.5)	16 (32.7)	8 (19.1)	12 (19.3)	8 (14.2)	3 (30.0)
7 – 8	1 (11.1)	3 (9.7)	--	10 (20.5)	3 (7.1)	7 (11.2)	4 (7.2)	1 (10.0)
8 – 9	--	1 (3.2)	--	4 (8.1)	2 (4.7)	1 (1.6)	2 (3.6)	--
10 & above	--	--	--	1 (2.0)	--	--	2 (3.6)	--
Total	*9 (100.00)*	*31 (100.00)*	*9 (100.00)*	*49 (100.00)*	*42 (100.00)*	*62 (100.00)*	*56 (100.00)*	*10 (100.00)*

Source : Primary data collected through field study. (Figures in the parantheses represent percent to the total)

Table 4.6 : Distribution of Non-Migrant Households According to Household Size

Household Size	*Baritola*	*B.P. Ladigam*	*Khamarigam*	*Onangpur*	*Bangarada*	*Mangalpur*	*Munigadi*	*Malati*	*Total*
Upto 3	3 (33.3)	6 (19.4)	3 (33.3)	7 (14.3)	8 (19.1)	12 (19.3)	4 (7.2)	5 (62.5)	48 (18.0)
4 – 5	4 (44.5)	14 (45.2)	4 (44.5)	16 (32.7)	12 (28.6)	18 (19.1)	13 (23.2)	2 (25.0)	83 (31.2)
6 – 7	1 (11.1)	8 (25.8)	1 (11.1)	14 (28.6)	11 (26.2)	7 (11.2)	9 (16.1)	1 (12.5)	52 (19.5)
7 – 8	1 (11.1)	2 (6.4)	--	3 (6.1)	6 (14.3)	9 (14.5)	10 (17.8)	--	31 (11.7)
8 – 9	--	1 (3.2)	1 (11.1)	6 (12.2)	2 (4.7)	11 (17.8)	8 (14.3)	--	29 (10.9)
10 and above	--	--	--	3 (6.1)	3 (7.1)	5 (8.1)	12 (21.4)	--	23 (8.7)
Total	*9 (100.00)*	*31 (100.00)*	*9 (100.00)*	*49 (100.00)*	*42 (100.00)*	*62 (100.00)*	*56 (100.00)*	*8 (100.00)*	*266 (100.00)*

(Figures in the parantheses represent percent to the total)

Table 4.7 : Distribution of Migrant Households on the Basis of Caste-composition

Caste	*Baritola*	*B.P. Ladigam*	*Khamarigam*	*Onangpur*	*Bangarada*	*Mangalpur*	*Munigadi*	*Malati*	*Total*
Scheduled Tribe (ST)	--	--	--	--	--	--	--	--	--
Scheduled Caste (SC)	--	4 (12.9)	--	24 (49.0)	12 (28.6)	11 (17.7)	13 (23.2)	9 (90.0)	73 (27.2)
Other Castes (OC)	9 (100.0)	27 (87.1)	9 (100.0)	25 (51.0)	30 (71.4)	51 (82.3)	43 (76.8)	1 (10.0)	195 (72.8)
Total	9 *(100.00)*	31 *(100.00)*	9 *(100.00)*	49 *(100.00)*	42 *(100.00)*	62 *(100.00)*	56 *(100.00)*	8 *(100.00)*	266 *(100.00)*

(Figures in the parantheses represent percent to the total)

(general category and other backward castes). The percentage of Scheduled castes from among all migrant households constitutes 27.2 which indicates the dominance of other castes migrant households (72.8%). It is revealed that in two villages Baritola and Khamarigam all migrant households are belonging to other castes. The scheduled caste migrant households constitute 90 percent in Malati followed by Onangapur (49.0 percent).

On the contrary, Table 4.8 illustrates the caste-composition of non-migrant households which is mainly in the category of Scheduled castes and other castes (General and other backward castes). The percentage of Scheduled castes from among all non-migrant households constitutes 26.69 which indicates the dominance of other castes non-migrant households (73.30%). It is found that all the non-migrant households of Khamarigam belong to the category of other castes. Similarly, all the non-migrant-households of Malati village belong to the category of scheduled castes.

Age Group of the Migrants

Age group of migrants are important from parlance of demographic and economic point of view as it has its impact on fertility, labour productivity and utilisation of human resources. It is worthwhile to note here that around 90 percent of migrants of all villages are in the age group of 15 to 45 years, out of which between 26 to 35 age group represents the highest percent (42.2%) followed by 15-25 age-group (25.9%). Below 14 year of age and above 46 years of age group of migrant represent a meagre percent of 3% and 6% respectively of the total migrants (Table 4.9).

The village-wise data highlight that four villages (Baritola, Khamarigam, K. Bangarada and Malati) child migrants are absent. A maximum percent of 43.4 and minimum percent of 20.0 of migrants belonging to age-group of 15 to 25 are from village Onangpur and Malati respectively. Two villages Khamarigam and Mangalpur represent equal percent of migrants (54.5%) in the age of group of 26 to 35 which is also the highest from among all migrants of all the villages of the said age group. Ten percent and above migrants in the age group of 46 plus are found in Malati and Munigadi.

Marital Status of Migrants

Table 4.10 depicts the marital status of migrants of the total migrants

Table 4.8 : Distribution of Non-Migrant Households on the Basis of Caste-Composition

Caste	*Baritola*	*B.P. Ladigam*	*Khamarigam*	*Onangpur*	*Bangarada*	*Mangalpur*	*Munigadi*	*Malati*	*Total*
Scheduled Tribe (ST)	--	--	--	--	--	--	--	--	--
Scheduled Caste (SC)	1 (11.1)	5 (16.1)	--	18 (36.7)	11 (26.2)	14 (22.6)	14 (25.0)	8 (100.00)	71 (26.69)
Other Castes (OC)	8 (88.9)	26 (83.9)	9 (100.00)	31 (63.3)	31 (73.8)	48 (77.4)	42 (75.0)	--	195 (73.30)
Total	*9 (100.00)*	*31 (100.00)*	*9 (100.00)*	*49 (100.00)*	*42 (100.00)*	*62 (100.00)*	*56 (100.00)*	*8 (100.00)*	*266 (100.00)*

(Figures in the parantheses represent percent to the total)

Table 4.9 : Distribution of Migrants according to their Age

Age-Group	*Baritola*	*B.P. Ladigam*	*Khamarigam*	*Onangpur*	*Bangarada*	*Mangalpur*	*Munigadi*	*Malati*	*Total*
0 – 14	--	1 (2.9)	--	3 (5.7)	-- (6.1)	4 (1.7)	1	--	9 (3.1)
15 – 25	4 (33.3)	9 (25.7)	2 (18.2)	23 (43.4)	20 (42.6)	4 (6.1)	12 (20.0)	2 (20.0)	76 (25.9)
26 – 35	4 (33.3)	12 (34.3)	6 (54.5)	19 (35.8)	15 (31.9)	36 (54.5)	28 (46.7)	4 (40.0)	124 (42.2)
36 – 45	3 (25.0)	10 (28.6)	3 (27.3)	4 (7.5)	12 (25.5)	18 (27.2)	12 (20.0)	3 (30.0)	65 (22.1)
46 +	1 (8.4)	3 (8.5)	--	4 (7.6)	--	4 (6.1)	7 (11.6)	1 (10.0)	20 (6.8)
Total	*12* *(100.00)*	*35* *(100.00)*	*11* *(100.00)*	*53* *(100.00)*	*47* *(100.00)*	*66* *(100.00)*	*60* *(100.00)*	*10* *(100.00)*	*294* *(100.00)*

(Figures in the parantheses represent percent to the total)

Table 4.10 : Distribution of Migrants According to their Marital Status

Marital Status	Baritola	B.P. Ladigam	Khamarigam	Onangpur	Bangarada	Mangalpur	Munigadi	Malati	Total
Married	6 (50.0)	15 (42.9)	5 (45.5)	28 (52.8)	28 (59.6)	31 (47.0)	31 (51.7)	5 (50.0)	149 (50.7)
Unmarried	5 (41.7)	9 (54.3)	6 (55.5)	23 (43.4)	18 (38.3)	34 (51.5)	27 (45.0)	5 (50.0)	137 (46.6)
Widow/ Divorcee	1 (8.3)	1 (2.8)	--	2 (3.8)	1 (2.1)	1 (1.5)	2 (3.3)	--	8 (2.7)
Total	*12 (100.00)*	*35 (100.00)*	*11 (100.00)*	*53 (100.00)*	*47 (100.00)*	*66 (100.00)*	*60 (100.00)*	*10 (100.00)*	*294 (100.00)*

(Figures in the parantheses represent percent to the total)

50.7 percent are married, 46.6 percent are unmarried and 2.7 percent are widower/divorcee.

More than half of migrants are married belonging to Baritola and Malati(50.0%), Munigadi(51.7%), Onangapur(52.8%) and K. Bangarada (59.6%). The villages reporting more than half of migrants unmarried belonging to Malati (50.0%, Mangalpur (51.5), B. Padmanavpur (54.3%) and Khamarigam (55.5%).

Place of Destination of the Migrants

Table 4.11 demonstrates information regarding place of destination of migrants. It is found that except B. Padmanavpur and Onangapur, no other village has migrants moving with in the state (outside the district). Further, it is revealed that only in B. Padamanavpur 11.4 percent of migrants move to rural areas with in the state (Outside the district and also having highest percent of migrants (80.0%) belonging to "within the state".

"Outside the state" 100 percentage of flow of migrants have been manifested in six villages to urban areas. The villages are Baritola, Khamarigam, Bangarada, Mangalpur, Munigadi, Malati. Migration to rural areas outside the state is the highest in the village Khamarigam (27.3 percent) followed by Munigadi (20%).

Main Reason of Migration

The main motive of migration as reported by households are depicted in Table 4.12. Divergent reasons are reported even from the same household having two migrant workmen. It is inferred from the table that research for livelihood is the dominant motive force of migration (30.3%) followed by unemployment (23.2%), drought, flood and other natural calamities (11.2%). Probably the recent flood in Ganjam and more particularly Aska and Digapahandi block (November 1990) has pushed migrants to leave their native village. One of the important factors responsible for migration is poverty (12.2%).

Number of Time(s) Migrated

Table 4.13 shows the number of times migrated by the migrants. It is found that the migrants for Third time constituted 22.1 percent from among all the migrants of all villages. In the village Malati Migrants for

Table 4.11 : Distribution of Migrants According to their Place of Destination

	Destination	*Baritola*	*B.P. Ladigam*	*Khamarigam*	*Onangpur*	*Bangarada*	*Mangalpur*	*Munigadi*	*Malati*	*Total*
Outside the District within the State	Total	--	28 (80.0)	--	16 (30.2)	--	--	--	--	44 (15.0)
	Rural	--	4 (11.4)	--	--	--	--	--	--	4 (9.0)
	Urban	--	24 (8.6)	--	16 (30.2)	--	--	--	--	40 (91.0)
	Total	**12** *(100.00)*	**7** *(100.00)*	**11** *(100.00)*	**37** *(100.00)*	**47** *(100.00)*	**66** *(100.00)*	**60** *(100.00)*	**10** *(100.00)*	**250** *(100.00)*
Outside the State	Rural	2 (16.7)	1 (2.9)	3 (27.3)	2 (3.8)	--	--	12 (20.0)	--	20 (8.0)
	Urban	10 (83.3)	6 (17.1)	8 (72.7)	35 (66.0)	47 (100.0)	66 (100.0)	48 (80.0)	10.0 (100.0)	230 (92.0)
	All Total	*12 (100.00)*	*35 (100.00)*	*11 (100.00)*	*53 (100.00)*	*47 (100.00)*	*66 (100.00)*	*60 (100.00)*	*10 (100.00)*	*294* **(100.00)**

(Figures in the parantheses represent percent to the total)

Table 4.12 : Distribution of Migrant Households according to their Main Reason of Migration

Reasons	*Baritola*	*B.P. Ladigam*	*Khamarigam*	*Onangpur*	*Bangarada*	*Mangalpur*	*Munigadi*	*Malati*	*Total*
Poverty	1 (8.3)	6 (17.1)	1 (9.1)	10 (18.9)	2 (4.3)	6 (9.1)	9 (15.0)	1 (10.0)	36 (12.2)
Unemployment	1 (16.7)	6 (17.1)	7 (63.6)	5 (9.4)	25 (53.2)	12 (18.2)	11 (18.3)	--	68 (23.2)
Search of Livelihood	6 (50.0)	12 (34.3)	--	18 (34.0)	5 (10.6)	23 (34.9)	18 (30.0)	7 (70.0)	89 (30.3)
Debt Bondage	1 (8.3)	6 (17.1)	1 (9.1)	7 (13.2)	2 (4.3)	1 (1.5)	3 (5.0)	2 (20.0)	23 (7.8)
Compelled by Advance Taken	1 (8.3)	3 (8.6)	--	1 (1.9)	--	--	2 (3.3)	--	7 (2.4)
Monotony of Rural Life	--	--	1 (9.1)	1 (1.9)	3 (6.4)	1 (1.5)	--	--	6 (2.0)
High hopes for future Better wages	--	--	--	--	10 (21.3)	15 (22.7)	7 (10.6)	--	32 (10.9)
Drought, flood and other natural calamities	1 (8.4)	2 (5.8)	1 (9.1)	11 (20.7)	--	8 (12.1)	10 (16.7)	--	33 (11.2)
Total	*12* *(100.00)*	*35* *(100.00)*	*11* *(100.00)*	*53* *(100.00)*	*47* *(100.00)*	*66* *(100.00)*	*60* *(100.00)*	*10* *(100.00)*	*294* *(100.00)*

(Figures in the parantheses represent percent to the total)

Table 4.13 : Distribution of Migrants on the Basis of Number of Times Migrated

No. of times migrated	*Baritola*	*B.P. Ladigam*	*Khamarigam*	*Onangpur*	*Bangarada*	*Mangalpur*	*Munigadi*	*Malati*	*Total*
First	1 (8.3)	3 (8.6)	2 (18.2)	2 (3.8)	3 (6.4)	4 (6.1)	3 (5.0)	2 (20.0)	20 (6.8)
Second	2 (16.7)	3 (8.6)	2 (18.2)	2 (3.8)	2 (4.3)	12 (18.2)	6 (10.0)	4 (40.0)	33 (11.2)
Third	3 (25.0)	8 (22.9)	2 (18.2)	16 (30.2)	14 (29.8)	10 (15.2)	8 (13.3)	4 (40.0)	65 (22.1)
Fourth	2 (16.7)	5 (14.3)	1 (9.0)	14 (26.4)	9 (19.1)	20 (30.3)	7 (11.7)	---	58 (19.7)
Fifth	4 (33.3)	10 (28.7)	2 (18.2)	6 (11.3)	7 (14.9)	17 (25.7)	11 (8.3)	---	57 (19.3)
Sixth or more	---	6 (17.1)	2 (18.2)	13 (24.5)	12 (25.5)	3 (4.5)	25 (41.7)	---	61 (20.7)
Total	*12* *(100.00)*	*35* *(100.00)*	*11* *(100.00)*	*53* *(100.00)*	*47* *(100.00)*	*66* *(100.00)*	*60* *(100.00)*	*10* *(100.00)*	*294* *(100.00)*

(Figures in the parantheses represent percent to the total)

fourth time and in the village Baritola migrants for sixth time were not found one third of migrants were migrated for fifth time in the village Baritola. More than 30 percent of migrants migrated for third and fourth times from the villages Onangapur (30.2%) and Mangalpur (30.3%) respectively. Munigadi village represents the highest percentage of migrants (41.7%) migrated for sixth or more times which is also the highest from among all the villages.

Duration of Migration

Table 4.14 unfolds the duration of migration among the migrants. Duration of migration for a period ranging from 3 to 4 years constitutes the highest percentage (24.8%) among the migrants of all villages. And lowest of 6.4 percent for a less than one year. The village level information reveal that migrants less than one year are not found in Mangalpur. Similarly, Migrants for a period of more than 3 years and more than 4 years are not found in the village Malati and Khamarigam respectively. It is interesting to note that migrants for more than 5 years constitute the highest percentage (36.6%) in the village Munigadi followed by Onangapur (24.5%) from among the villages. Similarly, migrants for a period of ranging from 3 to 4 years constituted highest percentage in the K. Bangarada (38.3%), followed by Onangapur (34.0%) from among the villages. The village Baritola represents the highest percentage of migrants (33.3%) for a period of 1 to 2 years.

Occupational Pattern

It is apparent from the Table 4.15 that Khamarigam village has the maximum percent (55.6%) of migrant households whose main occupation is cultivation. All the migrant households of Malati are Agricultural labourers. B. Padmanavpur occupies Second position (90.3%) regarding on occupational category of Agricultural labourers among the migrant households of all the villages. All remaining migrant households of except Khamarigam have more the 70 percent of households in the group of agricultural labourers. Household industry and other workers are conspicuously absent in the villages like Baritola, B. Padmanavpur, Khamarigam and Malati. Proportionately, a lower percent of migrant households are in this categories in the remaining villages.

A comparative picture of occupational pattern of non-migrant households is analysed in the Table 4.16. It is seen in the table that among the non-

Table 4.14 : Distribution of Migrants on the Basis of Duration (How long they have been migrated)

Duration	*Baritola*	*B.P. Ladigam*	*Khamarigam*	*Onangpur*	*Bangarada*	*Mangalpur*	*Munigadi*	*Malati*	*Total*
Less than one year	1 (8.3)	3 (8.6)	3 (27.3)	2 (3.8)	3 (6.4)	--	5 (8.3)	2 (20.0)	19 (6.4)
1 to 2 year	4 (33.3)	7 (20.0)	3 (27.3)	1 (1.9)	3 (6.4)	7 (10.6)	14 (23.4)	3 (30.0)	42 (14.2)
2 to 3 years	2 (16.7)	5 (14.3)	2 (18.1)	3 (5.7)	7 (14.9)	8 (12.1)	11 (18.3)	5 (50.0)	42 (14.6)
3 to 4 years	3 (25.5)	8 (22.9)	3 (27.3)	18 (34.0)	18 (38.3)	18 (27.3)	5 (8.3)	---	73 (24.8)
4 to 5 years	2 (16.7)	6 (17.1)	---	16 (30.2)	10 (21.3)	21 (31.8)	3 (5.0)	---	58 (19.7)
5 year or above	--	6 (17.1)	--	13 (24.5)	6 (12.,7)	12 (18.2)	22 (36.7)	---	59 (20.0)
Total	*12 (100.00)*	*35 (100.00)*	*11 (100.00)*	*53 (100.00)*	*47 (100.00)*	*66 (100.00)*	*60 (100.00)*	*10 (100.00)*	*294 (100.00)*

(Figures in the parantheses represent percent to the total)

Table 4.15 : Occupational Distribution of Migrant Households

Occupation	*Baritola*	*B.P. Ladigam*	*Khamarigam*	*Onangpur*	*Bangarada*	*Mangalpur*	*Munigadi*	*Malati*	*Total*
Cultivators	2 (22.2)	3 (9.7)	5 (55.6)	4 (8.2)	4 (9.5)	8 (12.9)	7 (12.5)	---	33
Agricultural labourers	7 (77.8)	28 (90.3)	4 (44.4)	38 (77.5)	32 (76.2)	48 (77.4)	41 (73.2)	10 (100.0)	208
Household Industries	---	---	---	3 (6.11)	2 (4.8)	2 (3.2)	3 (5.4)	---	10
Other Workers Business, etc.	---	---	---	4 (8.2)	4 (9.5)	4 (6.5)	5 (8.9)	---	17
Total	*9 (100.00)*	*31 (100.00)*	*9 (100.00)*	*49 (100.00)*	*42 (100.00)*	*62 (100.00)*	*56 (100.00)*	*10 (100.00)*	*268 (100.00)*

(Figures in the parantheses represent percent to the total)

Table 4.16 : Occupational Distribution of Non-Migrant Households

Occupation	*Baritola*	*B.P. Ladigam*	*Khamarigam*	*Onangpur*	*Bangarada*	*Mangalpur*	*Munigadi*	*Malati*	*Total*
Cultivators	5 (55.6)	8 (25.8)	4 (44.5)	11 (22.4)	10 (23.8)	28 (45.2)	27 (48.2)	7 (48.2)	100 (87.5)
Agricultural labourers	4 (44.4)	22 (71.0)	3 (33.3)	36 (73.5)	28 (66.7)	26 (41.9)	24 (42.9)	---	143 (53.8)
Household Industries	---	---	---	---	--	2 (3.2)	2 (3.6)	---	4 (1.5)
Other Workers Business, etc.	---	1 (3.2)	2 (22.2)	2 (4.1)	4 (9.5)	6 (9.7)	3 (5.3)	1 (12.5)	19 (7.1)
Total	*9 (100.00)*	*31 (100.00)*	*9 (100.00)*	*49 (100.00)*	*42 (100.00)*	*62 (100.00)*	*56 (100.00)*	*8 (100.00)*	*266 (100.00)*

(Figures in the parantheses represent percent to the total)

migrant households village Malati has the highest percent of cultivators (87.5 percent) followed by Baritola (55.6 percent). Agricultural labour households constitute 73.5 percent in Onangapur followed by B. Padmanavpur. In the category of occupation like "Other works, business," the village Khamarigam has 22.2 percent of non-migrant households.

Holding Size

Table 4.17 depicted the size of operational holding of the migrant households. It is revealed from the table that the landless migrant households constitute 100 percent in the village Malati, whereas it is lowest in both the villages of Baritola and Khamarigam (11.1%). So far as marginal operational holding are concerned, the migrant households of Onangapur constitute highest (69.4%) followed by Baritola 966.7%). More than half of the migrant households of K. Bangarada (57.1 percent) and B. Padmanavpur (58.1%) are belonging to the category of marginal holding. Migrant households of only three village i.e. Khamarigam (11.1%), K. Bangarada (2.4%) and Munigadi (5.4%) are having big holding.

The operational holding of non-migrant sample households is revealed in Table 4.18. It is manifested from the table that the landless non-migrant households constitute 100 percent in the village Malati where as it is the lowest in village Baritola (11.1%). So for as marginal operational holdings are concerned, the non-migrant households of Onangapur constitute the highest (55.1 percent) followed by K. Bangarada (52.4%). More than 10% of the households of Onangapur (10.2%), Mangalpur (11.3%) and Munigadi (12.5%) are having medium size of land holding where as big land holding households are totally absent in all the villages studied from among the non-migrant households.

Media of Migration

Table 4.19 illustrates the media of migrant workmen to the place of destination. The response of the migrant labourers show that more than 48 percent of migrants have gone to the destination place after receiving information though friends and relatives. Village-wise data reveal that in Khamarigam more than 72 percent of migrant could be migrated through their own initiative. While no one has been migrated through contractors, more than 11.5 percent of migrants have been migrated through unlicensed agents.

Table 4.17 : Distribution of Migrant Households According to the Size of the Operational Holdings

Land Holding	*Baritola*	*B.P. Ladigam*	*Khamarigam*	*Onangpur*	*Bangarada*	*Mangalpur*	*Munigadi*	*Malati*	*Total*
Landless Households	1 (11.1)	10 (32.3)	1 (11.1)	11 (22.4)	11 (31.0)	18 (29.0)	19 (33.9)	10 (100.0)	83 (31.0)
Marginal holding (Below 1 Hect.)	6 (66.7)	18 (58.1)	3 (33.4)	34 (69.4)	24 (57.1)	26 (41.9)	14 (25.0)	---	125 (46.7)
Small-holding (1–2 Hect.)	2 (22.2)	3 (9.6)	3 (33.3)	3 (6.1)	3 (7.1)	12 (19.4)	8 (14.3)	---	34 (12.7)
Medium-holding (2-4 hect.)	---	---	1 (11.1)	1 (2.1)	1 (2.4)	6 (9.7)	12 (21.4)	---	21 (7.8)
Big holding (4 – 8 Hect.)	---	---	1 (11.1)	---	1 (2.4)	---	3 (5.4)	---	5 (1.8)
Total	*9 (100.00)*	*31 (100.00)*	*9 (100.00)*	*49 (100.00)*	*42 (100.00)*	*62 (100.00)*	*56 (100.00)*	*10 (100.00)*	*268 (100.00)*

(Figures in the parantheses represent percent to the total)

Table 4.18 : Distributory of Non-migrant Households according to the size of the Operational Holding

Size of Holding	*Baritola*	*B.P. Ladigam*	*Khamarigam*	*Onangpur*	*Bangarada*	*Mangalpur*	*Munigadi*	*Malati*	*Total*
Landless	1 (11.1)	9 (29.0)	3 (33.3)	12 (24.5)	12 (28.6)	16 (25.8)	14 (25.0)	8 (100.0)	75 (28.2)
Marginal Holding	3 (33.3)	14 (45.2)	4 (44.5)	27 (55.1)	22 (52.4)	21 (33.9)	17 (30.4)	---	108 (40.6)
Small holding	5 (55.6)	8 (25.8)	2 (22.2)	5 (10.2)	8 (19.0)	18 (29.0)	18 (32.1)	---	64 (24.0)
Medium holding	---	---	--	5 (10.2)	---	7 (11.3)	7 (12.5)	---	19 (7.2)
Big holding	---	---	---	---	---	---	---	---	---
Total	*9* *(100.00)*	*31* *(100.00)*	*9* *(100.00)*	*49* *(100.00)*	*42* *(100.00)*	*62* *(100.00)*	*56* *(100.00)*	*8* *(100.00)*	*266* *(100.00)*

(Figures in the parantheses represent percent to the total)

Table 4.19 : Distribution of Migrants According to their Media of Migration

Migration Media	*Baritola*	*B.P. Ladigam*	*Khamarigam*	*Onangpur*	*Bangarada*	*Mangalpur*	*Munigadi*	*Malati*	*Total*
Own Initiative	8 (66.7)	22 (62.9)	8 (72.7)	26 (49.1)	18 (38.3)	16 (24.2)	11 (18.3)	7 (70.0)	116 (39.45)
Contractors	---	---	---	---	---	---	---	---	---
Unlicensed Agents	---	4 (11.4)	---	5 (9.4)	8 (17.0)	9 (13.6)	6 (10.0)	2 (20.0)	34 (11.56)
Through Friends and Relatives	4 (33.3)	9 (25.7)	3 (27.3)	20 (37.7)	21 (44.7)	41 (62.2)	43 (71.7)	1 (10.0)	142 (48.30)
Any Other	---	---	---	2 (3.8)	---	---	---	---	2 (0.60)
Total	*12 (100.00)*	*35 (100.00)*	*11 (100.00)*	*53 (100.00)*	*47 (100.00)*	*66 (100.00)*	*60 (100.00)*	*10 (100.00)*	*294 (100.00)*

(Figures in the parantheses represent percent to the total)

Level of Awareness

Awareness of migrant and non-migrant households have been represented in Table 4.20, which clearly demonstrates that migrant households are more conscious of various social problems and benefits of family planning and education compared to non-migrant households. This finding of the study is crystal clear in case of village level data collected in respect of Malati, Baritola, B. Padamanavpur Ladigam, Munigadi village.

Annual Income of Migrant and Non-migrant Households

Table 4.21 and 4.22 explaining the annual income of migrant and non-migrant households. Comparatively the non-migrant households are better off than migrant households. The data pertaining to their household income show that the migrant households in the annual income group of below Rs. 9,000 are 30.6 per cent where as the migrant households in the same income group are having as high as 52.3 percent. Similarly 15.4 percent of non-migrant household are in the income slab of 12,000 to Rs. 18,000 where as the migrant households constitute 6.7 percent in the same category. Thus, it can be inferred that the well-to-do non-migrant households are not preferring to migration.

Income and Expenditure of Migrants

Table 4.23 and 4.24 exhibits the income and expenditure of migrants at their place of destination. Most of the migrants (65.7 percent) are within the average annual income group of Rs. 17,000/- migrants in the average annual income of Rs. 9000 to Rs. 12,000 is 26.2 percent and slightly less percent (25.2%) are in the average annual income limit of Rs. 9,000 to Rs. 17,000/-. Similarly, migrants of B. Padmanavpur are earning below the annual income of Rs. 20,000/-. In the highest income group of Rs. 21,000/ - and above, these are only three villages K. Bangarada (4.3%), Mangalpur (7.6%) and Munigadi (3.4%), combinedly constitute 3 per cent of the total migrants.

With regard to expenditure, maximum percent of migrants about 80 percent are incurring annual expenditure with in Rs. 7,000/-. The lowest percent of 2.7 percent of migrants are spending Rs. 10,000/- and above annually.

All migrants of villages Baritola, B. Padmanavpur, Onangapur and Malati are spending annual expenditure below Rs. 7,000/- and migrants

Table 4.20 : Percentage Distribution of Migrant Households (M.H.) and Non-migrant Households (N.M.H.) on the Basis of Their Awareness

Villages	Awareness about family planning		Interest for education		Social awareness about dowry system		Health Care		Awareness about AIDS		Awareness about Smoking, Wine	
	M.H.	N.M.H.	M.H.	N.M.H.	M.H.	N.M.H.	M..H.	N.M.H.	M.H.H.	N.M.H.	M.H.	N.M.H.
Baritola	6 (66.6)	5 (55.5)	6 (66.6)	3 (33.3)	5 (55.5)	4 (44.4)	4 (44.4)	3 (33.3)	3 (33.3)	2 (22.2)	7 (77.7)	4 (44.4)
B.P.-Ladigam	24 (77.4)	26 (83.8)	16 (51.6)	10 (32.2)	17 (54.8)	14 (45.1)	10 (32.2)	08 (25.8)	5 (16.1)	12 (38.7)	25 (80.6)	16 (51.6)
Khamarigam	5 (53.5)	5 (55.5)	4 (44.4)	6 (66.6)	3 (33.3)	5 (55.5)	4 (44.4)	3 (33.3)	3 (33.3)	4 (44.4)	5 (55.5)	4 (44.4)
Onangpur	30 (61.2)	36 (73.4)	25 (51.0)	25 (51.0)	18 (36.7)	20 (40.8)	15 (30.6)	18 (36.7)	12 (24.4)	15 (30.6)	38 (77.5)	30 (61.2)
Bangarada	26 (61.9)	20 (47.6)	12 (28.5)	15 (35.7)	18 (42.8)	20 (47.6)	18 (42.8)	15 (35.7)	15 (35.7)	10 (23.8)	28 (66.6)	18 (42.8)
Mangalpur	38 (61.2)	30 (48.3)	28 (45.1)	30 (48.3)	30 (48.3)	20 (32.2)	17 (27.4)	20 (32.2)	20 (32.2)	15 (24.1)	42 (67.4)	32 (51.6)
Munigadi	40 (71.4)	28 (50.0)	24 (42.8)	26 (46.4)	28 (50.0)	15 (26.7)	20 (35.7)	18 (32.1)	22 (39.3)	12 (21.4)	42 (75.0)	30 (53.5)
Malati	8 (80.0)	5 (62.5)	4 (40.0)	4 (50.0)	6 (60.0)	4 (50.0)	5 (50.0)	3 (37.5)	5 (50.0)	3 (37.)	8 (80.0)	5 (62.5)

(Figures in the parantheses represent percent to the total)

Table 4.21 : Distribution of Migrants Households According to their Annual Income (including remittances)

Incomes (Rs.)	*Baritola*	*B.P. Ladigam*	*Khamarigam*	*Onangpur*	*Bangarada*	*Mangalpur*	*Munigadi*	*Malati*	*Total*
Below Rs.9,000	2 (22.2)	4 (12.9)	---	32 (65.3)	16 (38.1)	18 (29.0)	4 (7.1)	6 (60.0)	82 (30.6)
Rs. 9,000 to Rs. 12,000	4 (44.5)	17 (54.8)	4 (44.4)	10 (20.4)	15 (35.7)	12 (19.4)	10 (17.9)	3 (30.0)	75 (28.0)
Rs. 12,000 to Rs. 18,000	3 (33.3)	8 (25.8)	4 (44.5)	7 (14.3)	11 (26.2)	28 (45.2)	28 (50.0)	1 (10.0)	90 (33.6)
Rs. 18,000 to Rs. 22,000	---	1 (3.2)	1 (1.1)	---	---	2 (3.2)	14 (25.0)	---	18 (6.7)
Rs. 22,000 and above	---	1 (3.3)	---	---	---	2 (3.2)	---	---	3 (1.1)
Total	*9* *(100.00)*	*31* *(100.00)*	*9* *(100.00)*	*49* *(100.00)*	*42* *(100.00)*	*62* *(100.00)*	*56* *(100.00)*	*10* *(100.00)*	*268* *(100.00)*

(Figures in the parantheses represent percent to the total)

Table 4.22 : Distribution of Non-Migrants Households on the basis of their Annual Income (including remittances)

Income (Rs.)	*Baritola*	*B.P. Ladigam*	*Khamarigam*	*Onangpur*	*Bangarada*	*Mangalpur*	*Munigadi*	*Malati*	*Total*
Below Rs.9,000	4 (44.5)	19 (61.3)	4 (44.4)	34 (69.4)	24 (57.1)	25 (40.3)	22 (39.3)	7 (87.5)	139 (52.3)
Rs. 9,000 to Rs. 12,000	2 (22.2)	8 (25.8)	1 (11.1)	9 (18.4)	8 (19.1)	33 (53.2)	21 (37.5)	--	82 (30.8)
Rs. 12,000 to Rs. 18,000	3 (33.3)	3 (9.7)	4 (44.5)	5 (10.2)	10 (23.8)	4 (6.5)	11 (19.6)	1 (12.5)	41 (15.4)
Rs. 18,000 to Rs. 22,000	---	1 (3.2)	---	1 (2.0)	---	---	2 (3.2)	---	4 (1.5)
Rs. 22,000 and above	---	---	---	---	---	---	---	---	---
Total	*9 (100.00)*	*31 (100.00)*	*9 (100.00)*	*49 (100.00)*	*42 (100.00)*	*62 (100.00)*	*56 (100.00)*	*8 (100.00)*	*266 (100.00)*

(Figures in the parantheses represent percent to the total)

Table 4.23 : Distribution of Non-Migrants Households on the basis of their Annual Income

Income (Rs.)	*Baritola*	*B.P. Ladigam*	*Khamarigam*	*Onangpur*	*Bangarada*	*Mangalpur*	*Munigadi*	*Malati*	*Total*
Below Rs.9,000	---	4 (11.4)	---	28 (52.8)	5 (10.6)	2 (3.0)	3 (5.0)	---	42 (14.3)
Rs. 9,000 to below Rs. 12,000	3 (25.0)	24 (68.6)	3 (27.3)	13 (24.5)	15 (31.9)	7 (10.6)	5 (8.3)	7 (70.0)	77 (26.2)
Rs. 12,000 to below Rs. 17,000	4 (33.3)	6 (17.1)	4 (36.4)	12 (22.7)	8 (17.0)	11 (16.7)	26 (43.3)	3 (30.0)	74 (25.20
Rs. 18,000 to below Rs. 20,000	3 (25.0)	1 (2.9)	3 (27.3)	---	7 (14.9)	27 (40.9)	20 (33.3)	---	61 (20.7)
Rs. 20,000 to below 20,000	2 (16.7)	---	1 (9.0)	---	10 (21.3)	14 (21.2)	4 (6.7)	---	31 (10.5)
Rs. 21,000 and above	---	---	---	---	2 (4.3)	5 (7.6)	2 (3.4)	---	9 (3.1)
Total	*12 (100.00)*	*35 (100.00)*	*11 (100.00)*	*53 (100.00)*	*47 (100.00)*	*66 (100.00)*	*60 (100.00)*	*10 (100.00)*	*294 (100.00)*

(Figures in the parantheses represent percent to the total)

Table 4.24 : Annual Expenditure of the Migrants at their Place of Destination (as reported by household members and migrants during their short visit to home)

Income (Rs.)	*Baritola*	*B.P. Ladigam*	*Khamarigam*	*Onangpur*	*Bangarada*	*Mangalpur*	*Munigadi*	*Malati*	*Total*
Below Rs.4,000	1 (8.3)	17 (48.6)	---	31 (58.5)	2 (4.3)	4 (6.1)	2 (3.3)	4 (40.0)	61 (20.7)
Rs. 4,000 to below Rs. 5,500	4 (33.3)	10 (28.6)	2 (18.2)	20 (37.7)	11 (23.4)	15 (22.7)	12 (20.0)	5 (50.0)	77 (26.9)
Rs. 5,500 to below Rs. 7,000	7 (58.4)	8 (22.8)	7 (63.6)	2 (3.8)	18 (38.3)	23 (34.8)	28 (46.7)	1 (10.0)	94 (32.0)
Rs. 7,000 to below Rs. 8,500	---	---	2 (18.2)	---	10 (21.3)	15 (22.7)	14 (23.3)	---	41 (14.0)
Rs. 8,500 to below Rs. 10,000	---	---	---	---	4 (8.5)	4 (6.1)	3 (5.0)	---	11 (3.7)
Rs. 10,000 and above	---	---	---	---	2 (4.2)	5 (7.6)	1 (1.7)	---	8 (2.7)
Total	*12 (100.00)*	*35 (100.00)*	*11 (100.00)*	*53 (100.00)*	*47 (100.00)*	*66 (100.00)*	*60 (100.00)*	*10 (100.00)*	*294 (100.00)*

(Figures in the parantheses represent percent to the total)

of Khamarigam are incurring expenditure less than Rs. 8,500/- during the year.

Migrants of K. Bangarada, (4.2%), Mangalpur (7.6) and Munigadi (1.7%) are spending Rs. 10,000 and above in a year constituted 2.7 percent of total migrants. Further, it is interesting to mention here that among the migrant villages all migrants of Khamarigam reported annual expenditure more than Rs. 4,000/- where as in all other villages there are migrants spending below Rs. 3,600 per annum.

Consumption Expenditure of the Household

Household average consumption expenditure of migrants and non-migrants have been expressed in Table 4.25 and 4.26. Most of the migrants (39.9) are in the average consumption expenditure of Rs. 4,000 to Rs. 4,500. In the village B. Padmanavpur, Onangpur and Malati all migrants' per capita annual average consumption expenditure is below 4,500. Similarly, in Baritola average per capita annual consumption expenditure is below Rs.5,000/-. In the village Khamarigam migrants spend per capita annual expenditure within the range of Rs.4,000 to Rs.5,500. The highest per capita expenditure of migrants are manifested only in three village K. Bangarad (7.2%), Mangalpur (8%) and Munigadi (10.7%), combinedly constitute 5.2 percent of the total migrant households.

Pertaining to per capita annual consumption expenditure of non-migrant households, more than half of non-migrant households, (52.6%) spend below Rs. 3,500/- within the expenditure slab of Rs.3,500 to Rs.4,000/- there are 94 non-migrant households which constitute 35.4 percent of the total non-migrant households. Thus, within Rs.4,000/- consumption expenditure there are 88 percent of households. Thus, it is demonstrated that compared to migrant households, the non-migrants' per capita annual consumption expenditure considerable low. This reflects the comparatively distressed condition of living standard of the non-migrant households. Only 11 households constituting 4.1 percent are incurring per capita annual consumption expenditure of Rs.5,000 to Rs.5,500/-.

It is seen from the interview schedules that the average migrants' expenditure include inter alia, purchase of goods like transistors, blankets, sarees, etc, during their return journey.

Table 4.25 : Per-capita Annual Average Consumption Expenditure of the Migrant Households

Income (Rs.)	*Baritola*	*B.P. Ladigam*	*Khamarigam*	*Onangpur*	*Bangarada*	*Mangalpur*	*Munigadi*	*Malati*	*Total*
Below Rs.3,500	1 (11.1)	2	---	3 (6.1)	1 (2.4)	1 (1.6)	3 (5.4)	1 (10.0)	12 (4.5)
Rs. 3,500 to below Rs. 4,000	3 (33.3)	22	---	22 (44.9)	4 (9.5)	7 (11.3)	12 (21.4)	7 (70.0)	77 (28.7)
Rs. 4,000 to below Rs. 4,500	1 (11.1)	7	4 (44.5)	24 (49.0)	9 (21.4)	15 (24.2)	18 (32.2)	2 (20.0)	80 (39.9)
Rs. 4,500 to below Rs. 5,000	4 (44.5)	---	3 (33.3)	---	15 (35.7)	23 (37.1)	12 (21.4)	---	57 (21.3)
Rs. 5,000 to below Rs. 5,500	---	---	2 (22.2)	---	10 (23.8)	11 (17.7)	5 (8.9)	---	28 (10.4)
Rs. 5,500 and above	---	---	---	---	3 (7.2)	5 (8.1)	6 (10.7)	---	14 (5.2)
Total	*9 (100.00)*	*31 (100.00)*	*9 (100.00)*	*49 (100.00)*	*42 (100.00)*	*62 (100.00)*	*56 (100.00)*	*10 (100.00)*	*268 (100.00)*

(Figures in the parantheses represent percent to the total)

Table 4.26 : Per-capita Annual Consumption Expenditure of the Non-Migrant Households

Income (Rs.)	*Baritola*	*B.P. Ladigam*	*Khamarigam*	*Onangpur*	*Bangarada*	*Mangalpur*	*Munigadi*	*Malati*	*Total*
Below Rs.3,500	4 (44.4)	21 (67.7)	4 (44.4)	34 (69.4)	24 (57.1)	24 (38.7)	22 (39.3)	7 (87.5)	140 (52.6)
Rs. 3,500 to below Rs. 4,000	4 (44.5)	2 (6.5)	5 (55.6)	11 (22.4)	11 (26.2)	34 (54.8)	26 (46.4)	1 (12.5)	94 (35.4)
Rs. 4,000 to below Rs. 4,500	1 (11.1)	6 (19.4)	---	3 (6.1)	3 (7.2)	2 (3.2)	6 (10.7)	---	21 (7.9)
Rs. 4,500 to below Rs. 5,000	---	2 (6.4)	---	1 (2.1)	4 (9.5)	2 (3.3)	2 (3.6)	---	11 (4.1)
Rs. 5,000 to Rs. 5,500	---	---	---	---	---	---	---	---	---
Rs. 5,500 and above	---	---	---	---	---	---	---	---	---
Total	*9 (100.00)*	*31 (100.00)*	*9 (100.00)*	*49 (100.00)*	*42 (100.00)*	*62 (100.00)*	*56 (100.00)*	*8 (100.00)*	*266 (100.00)*

(Figures in the parantheses represent percent to the total)

Consumption of fish, egg, good food, bearing good clothes, using radio-sets, tape recorder, etc. are noticed after the migrants return to their villages. Thus, the migrant households expenditure is comparatively higher to non-migrants.

Indebtedness

The indebted position of migrant and non-migrant households have been analysed in Table 4.27 and 4.28. It is seen in Table 4.27 that households without any debt constitute more than 55 percent among the migrants. Debt ranging from Rs. 1000 to Rs. 2000 constitute 27.2 percent of the total households. Thirteen migrant households, constituting 4.9 percent of the total house-holds and four households (1.5%) are within the debt range of Rs. 2,000 to Rs.4,000 and to Rs. 6000 respectively.

Extent of indebtedness of non-migrant households have been reflected in Table 4.28. It is found from the processed data that there are 81 no-debt households which constitute 30.5 percent compared to migrants, the position of non-migrants are somehow better. This is inferred from the percentage of debt households. Only six migrant households constituting 2.3 percent of the total are in the debt range of Rs. 4000 to above Rs.6000/- where as there are 43 non-migrant households (16.2%) are in the debt position of Rs.4000 to above Rs. 6000/-. Thus, non-migrants are more indebted compared to migrant households. This may be due to better capacity of migrants to clear off the debt through remittance. This is in tern, because of assured income position of migrant households through employment at the destination.

Remittances

Remittances by migrants to their households represented in Table 4.29 It is revealed that maximum percent 22.4% of the total migrants remitted Rs. 3000 to Rs.4000 per annum to their households. The migrants of Malati are remitting below Rs. 3000 per annum, where as the migrants of B. Padmanavapur, Onagpur remit below Rs.4,000 and below Rs. 5000 has been remitted by all migrants of Baritola and K. Bangarada. It is contrast to note that the migrants of Munigadi and Mangalpur are dispersed from no-remittance group to the highest remittance group. In both the villages of Mangalpur and Munigadi, migrants reported as not remitting any amount constitute 15.1 and 13.3 percent respectively.

Table 4.27 : Indebtedness of the Migrant Households

Magnitude of Debt (in Rs.)	*Baritola*	*B.P. Ladigam*	*Khamarigam*	*Onangpur*	*Bangarada*	*Mangalpur*	*Munigadi*	*Malati*	*Total*
No debt	2 (22.2)	14 (45.2)	4 (44.4)	37 (75.5)	16 (38.1)	36 (58.1)	33 (58.1)	6 (60.0)	148 (55.2)
Below Rs. 1,000	4 (44.5)	11 (31.4)	5 (55.6)	7 (14.3)	14 (33.3)	15 (24.2)	14 (25.0)	3 (30.0)	73 (27.2)
Rs. 1,000 to below Rs. 2,000	2 (22.2)	4 (12.9)	---	2 (4.1)	8 (19.0)	7 (11.3)	4 (7.1)	1 (10.0)	28 (10.4)
Rs. 2,000 to below Rs. 4,000	1 (11.1)	2 (6.5)	---	3 (6.1)	3 (7.2)	2 (3.2)	2 (1.8)	---	13 (1.5)
Rs. 4,000 to below Rs. 6,000	---	---	---	---	1 (2.4)	2 (3.2)	1 (1.8)	---	4 (1.5)
Rs. 6,000 and above	---	---	---	---	---	---	2 (3.6)	---	2 (0.8)
Total	*9 (100.00)*	*31 (100.00)*	*9 (100.00)*	*49 (100.00)*	*42 (100.00)*	*62 (100.00)*	*56 (100.00)*	*10 (100.00)*	*268 (100.00)*

(Figures in the parantheses represent percent to the total)

Table 4.28 : Indebtedness of the Non-Migrant Households

Magnitude of Debt (in Rs.)	*Baritola*	*B.P. Ladigam*	*Khamarigam*	*Onangpur*	*Bangarada*	*Mangalpur*	*Munigadi*	*Malati*	*Total*
No debt	3 (33.4)	5 (16.1)	3 (33.4)	13 (26.5)	12 (28.6)	16 (25.8)	25 (44.6)	4 (50.0)	81 (30.5)
Below Rs. 1,000	1 (11.1)	4 (12.9)	1 (11.1)	9 (18.4)	7 (16.7)	24 (38.7)	18 (32.1)	1 (12.5)	65 (24.4)
Rs.1,000 to below Rs. 2,000	2 (22.2)	2 (6.4)	3 (33.3)	5 (10.2)	21 (50.0)	2 (3.2)	5 (8.9)	1 (12.5)	41 (15.4)
Rs. 2,000 to below Rs. 4,000	1 (11.1)	7 (22.6)	---	13 (26.5)	2 (4.7)	11 (17.7)	2 (3.6)	---	36 (13.5)
Rs. 4,000 to below Rs. 6,000	1 (11.1)	10 (32.3)	1 (11.1)	2 (4.1)	---	4 (6.5)	2 (3.6)	1 (12.5)	21 (7.9)
Rs. 6,000 and above	1 (11.1)	3 (9.7)	1 (11.1)	7 (14.3)	---	5 (8.1)	4 (7.2)	1 (12.5)	22 (8.3)
Total	*9 (100.00)*	*31 (100.00)*	*9 (100.00)*	*49 (100.00)*	*42 (100.00)*	*62 (100.00)*	*56 (100.00)*	*8 (100.00)*	*266 (100.00)*

(Figures in the parantheses represent percent to the total)

Table 4.29 : Average Annual Remittances of the Migrants (in Cash) to their Households

Amount of Remittance (in Rs.)	*Baritola*	*B.P. Ladigam*	*Khamarigam*	*Onangpur*	*Bangarada*	*Mangalpur*	*Munigadi*	*Malati*	*Total*
No. of Remittance	---	---	---	---	---	10 (15.1)	8 (13.3)	--	--- (6.1)
Below Rs. 1,500	2 (16.7)	16 (45.7)	2 (18.1)	18 (34.0)	3 (6.4)	---	6 (10.0)	6 (60.0)	53 (18.0)
Rs. 1,500 to below Rs. 2,000	1 (8.3)	4 (11.4)	1 (9.1)	13 (24.5)	7 (14.8)	6 (9.0)	9 (15.0)	2 (20.0)	43 (14.6)
Rs. 2,000 to below Rs. 3,000	1 (8.3)	10 (28.5)	1 (9.1)	16 (30.2)	10 (20.4)	7 (10.6)	17 (28.4)	2 (20.0)	64 (21.8)
Rs. 3,000 to below Rs. 4,000	5 (41.7)	5 (14.4)	4 (36.4)	6 (11.3)	18 (38.3)	17 (28.3)	11 (18.3)	---	66 (22.4)
Rs. 4,000 to below Rs. 5,000	3 (25.0)	---	2 (18.2)	---	9 (19.1)	12 (18.1)	3 (5.0)	---	29 (9.9)
Rs. 5,000 to Rs. 6,000	---	---	1 (9.1)	---	---	5 (7.5)	2 (3.3)	---	8 (2.7)
Rs. 6,000 and above	---	---	---	---	---	9 (13.6)	4 (6.7)	---	13 (4.5)
Total	*12 (100.00)*	*35 (100.00)*	*11 (100.00)*	*53 (100.00)*	*47 (100.00)*	*66 (100.00)*	*60 (100.00)*	*10 (100.00)*	*294 (100.00)*

(Figures in the parantheses represent percent to the total)

In-conveniences of the Migrants

Work-environment has its impact on the flow of migrants to the work-site, health, efficiency and productivity. Therefore, it is pertinent to focus on the inconveniences faced by the migrants in their place of destination.

The return migrants reported (Table 4.30) that most of them (32 percent) are victimized by disease and health problems. More than 51 percent of migrants of Mangalpur have reported the disease and health problem at Surat and other places followed by Munigadi (36.7 percent). Out of 294 migrants, 144 migrants (48.9 percent) have reported adverse work environment. The village-wise analysis reveals that in K. Bangarada 32 migrants out of 47 constitute the highest of 68 percent have reported unhygenic work condition followed by Munigadi (50%) and Onangpur (49%). Moreover, ill-treatment of the employer has been reported by 10 migrants (3.4%) only.

Level of Education

It has been brought to light from Table 4.31 that migrants having primary level of education has the maximum percent (47.6%) whereas minimum of 1.4 percent of migrants are having higher secondary and above qualification. Illiterate migrants constitutes 21.4 per cent of all the villages. Most of the migrants of Onangpur (71.7) and Baritola (66.7) represents primary level of Education. Migrants of village Malati and Baritola do not have middle school and higher school level of education. However, more than one-third of migrants having middle school of education are found in villages Bangarada (38.3%), Khamarigam (36.4%) and B. Padmanavpur (34.3%).

The general conclusion which emerges from the study of migrant labour in Orissa is that although most of the migrants flow to Surat, they are also concentrated in construction, mining activities, earth-works etc.

In this context, the profile of Surat City—the destination of Oriya rural-migrant labourers is mention-worthy.

Surat

One of the largest and fastest growing cities in India is Surat. Its population has increased more than four times in the last three decades

Table 4.30 : Distribution of Migrants reported Inconveniences in their Place of Destination

Inconvenience	*Baritola*	*B.P. Ladigam*	*Khamarigam*	*Onangpur*	*Bangarada*	*Mangalpur*	*Munigadi*	*Malati*	*Total*
Long hours of work	2 (16.7)	8 (22.8)	3 (27.3)	5 (9.4)	---	---	2 (3.3)	3 (30.0)	23 (7.8)
Un-hygenic work condition	5 (41.7)	11 (31.4)	4 (36.3)	26 (49.0)	32 (68.0)	32 (48.5)	30 (50.0)	4 (40.0)	144 (48.9)
Illtreatment of the employer	---	3 (8.5)	1 (9.1)	1 (1.9)	---	---	4 (6.7)	1 (10.0)	10 (3.4)
Harassment in payment of wages..	1 (8.3)	7 (20.0)	1 (9.1)	7 (13.2)	5 (10.7)	---	2 (3.3)	---	23 (7.8)
Disease and health problems	4 (33.3)	6 (17.1)	2 (18.2)	14 (26.5)	10 (21.3)	34 (51..5)	22 (36.7)	2 (20.0)	94 (32.0)
Total	*12 (100.00)*	*35 (100.00)*	*11 (100.00)*	*53 (100.00)*	*47 (100.00)*	*66 (100.00)*	*60 (100.00)*	*10 (100.00)*	*294 (100.00)*

(Figures in the parantheses represent percent to the total)

Table 4.31 : Distribution of Migrants According to their Level of Education

Level of education	*Baritola*	*B.P. Ladigam*	*Khamarigam*	*Onangpur*	*Bangarada*	*Mangalpur*	*Munigadi*	*Malati*	*Total*
Illiterate	2 (16.7)	10 (28.6)	3 (27.3)	3 (5.7)	2 (4.3)	18 (27.3)	19 (31.7)	6 (60.0)	63 (21.4)
Primary	8 (66.7)	11 (31.4)	3 (27.3)	38 (71.7)	18 (38.3)	31 (47.0)	27 (45.0)	4 (40.0)	140 (49.6)
Middle School	2 (16.6)	12 (34.3)	4 (36.4)	9 (17.0)	18 (38.3)	9 (13.6)	8 (13.3)	---	62 (21.1)
High School	---	1 (2.8)	1 (9.1)	3 (5.6)	9 (19.1)	8 (12.1)	3 (5.0)	---	25 (8.5)
Higher Second-ary and above	---	1 (2.9)	---	---	---	---	3 (5.0)	---	4 (0.4)
Total	*12 (100.00)*	*35 (100.00)*	*11 (100.00)*	*53 (100.00)*	*47 (100.00)*	*66 (100.00)*	*60 (100.00)*	*10 (100.00)*	*294 (100.00)*

(Figures in the parantheses represent percent to the total)

from 3.71 Lakh in 1971, to 14.91 Lakh in 1991. During 1971, it was the 19th largest city in India but at present (1991), it occupies the 12th rank.[1]

Growth of Powerlooms in Surat Urban Agglomeration Area

Year	No. of Looms	Index of Growth
1950	2882	100
1960	8105	281
1970	19025	660
1980	25488	884
1990	200000	6939

Source : R.S. Gandhi, 1991. Published in Economic and Political Weekly, Oct. 8, 1994 p. 2672.

The increase in the population of Surat city is attributed to the factor like unprecedented growth of small-scale industries in unorganised sector.

Jari, handloom weaving or powerloom are the traditional industries have accelerated the growth of Surat. Jari is, however, confined to small sector. Diamond cutting and polishing are recent additions. And since the mid-805 large-scale petro-chemical industries have accelerated the growth of the city.

Surat is one of the largest centres in the country for production of synthetic fibre fabrics, mainly nylon and polyster.

In 1994, there were an estimated 2.5 lakh looms. A majority of the small Units are fabricated by owners to circulate the rule of the Factory Act. They divide ownership of looms in the names of existing or imaginary family members, though in all other respects looms operate and are managed by one family under one roof. This device is locally known as 'Bhagala' i.e. fragmentation system has come to dominate the industry. For instance, 41 percent of the Units in 1962 used to employ more than 50 labourers. Their number had gone down to 3 per cent in 1971–72.[2]

Alongwith, the weaving, dyeing and processing units generate huge amounts of black-money in the city, which makes living dearer for the common person.

Unhygienic Living Condition

The single largest problem mentioned by the poor as well as rich, males as well as females, locals and immigrants was the unhygienic condition of the city.

Though the labourers receive relatively more wages than they would receive in their place of origin (Ganjam District), their wages have non-increased correspondingly with price rise. Their working and living conditions are hazardous. They are susceptible to all types of diseases.

Lack of assured source of employment, frequent crop failures and expected increase in income motivate the rural households of Ganjam to migrate to Surat. They migrate alongwith their wives and children. Thus, there is oxdus of rural labour from Orissa, mostly from Ganjam district to Surat. Even one can notice migrant labourers from Andhra Pradesh, Bihar, Madhya Pradesh to Surat City.

Jan Breman has aptly remarked, "Surat is basically one big transit camp of labour coming-in and going-off again. Thus place is swamped with a floating mass which remains outside the land beyond the benign reach of state agencies. The transients are reduced to passing labour commodity in a cycle of attraction and rejection, condemned to a cite which is inhuman by any definition."[3]

As has been mentioned earlier, an important industry employing large-scale migrant labourers is diamond industry. There are more than 5,000 diamond cutting and polishing shops in the Surat city employing 8 to 10 workers in each Unit. This industry is totally dependent upon foreign countries for its market. These industries have attracted migrant workers not only from villages but also from other states like Rajasthan, Bihar, Orissa, Uttar Pradesh and Maharashtra.[4]

References

1. Shah Ghanashyam, *Economy and Civil Authority in Surat*, Economic and Political Weekly. Oct. 8, 1994, p. 2671.
2. *Ibid* p. 2672
3. Jan., Breman, *Economic and Political Weekly*, April, 17, 1993
4. Barik, B.C., *Rural Migrants in an Urban Setting*, Classical Publishing Company, New Delhi, 1994, p. 21.

5

Labour Migration and Its Impact

SECTION—A

At attempt has been made in this chapter to assess the impact of labour migration in the rural economy of Ganjam and also the study of linkages, as a result of migration. Section B of this chapter deals with concluding observations.

Migration of rural labourers to urban centres has far-reaching repercussions on the village economy. Migration has both economy and non-economic consequences which can be examined by analysing socio-economic linkages on different variables.

Utilisation of Physical and human resources results in economic development. Population growth unaccompanied by non-agricultural sector must lead to rural out-migration. Because, when dairying, poultry, forestry or cottage and small-scale industries to not expand so as to absorb the surplus labour, mounting number of people must move to urban centre for employment.

Unemployment and poverty in rural-economy is the result of multi-dimensional factors. Alongside growth of population, factors like low rate of investment in agriculture, inequalities in the distribution of land and other productive assets, lack of credit facilities to poor are some of the features aggravating rural unemployment. Apart from these, the capital-intensive technology used in agriculture replaces labour by the mechanization process. Access to institutional credit can solve the problems of rich landlords but the small and marginal farmers usually borrow from the non-institutional sources like moneylenders who charge usurious interest rates.

Rural economy has been linked with urban centres due to the development of transport and communication. As a result, the external forces have pretreated to rural economy. The growing demand for modern consumption goods and the availability of new capital intensive modes of production have led to shifts in production and subsistence to cash crops. This shift of paradigms further led to commercialization of agriculture, competition among rural producers, increased inequality in land distribution and ultimately, landlessness.

Sometimes Government policy influences the distribution of population between rural and urban areas. These include policies of concentrating industrial infrastructure in the cities, price and import and substitution policies oriented towards meeting urban consumption aspirations and wide range of social service investments in urban areas.

With regard to impact of migration, most studies based on survey data and field studies focused that migrants have been able to increase their welfare as a result of individual migrants and their families not only appear generally better off as a result of migration, but also seen be assimilated soon with socio-economic set up in urban areas.

On the basis of our study, let us review the impact of migration, under following heads.

Impact of Migration for Migrants and Their Households

The impact of migration and issues related to it are complex and complicated.

If the out-migrant is a dependent, either a child or an old person, unless funds are sent to that out-migrants, per capita consumption of remaining house hold member may rise. Because, there is one less person to consume but no decline in the labour input of remaining family members. But generally an out-migrants is an adult and able-bodied person who leaves the village to work. The less or absence of such a member due to migration, there will be a net loss in the household per consequences (ignoring the aspect of remittance for the time being).

i) Remaining household members in the village may respond to the reduced household labour supply by increasing their labour inputs to compensate, to maintain a balance in their living standard.

ii) Such a response is contingent upon the existence of so-called "disguised unemployment" in the household before, so the additional work effort is possible from existing members of the labour force. Alternatively, some re-allocation is possible within the household through children dropping out from school to work. Though increase in the hours of work by women and effecting their economic status some re-allocation of labour can be made to compensate the loss of labour inputs due to out-migration. The access to means of production (land or capital etc.) determines the extent to which remaining family members can increase their labour inputs. If the rural household has no such means and consists solely of wage labourers, then its opportunities for increasing work effort depend on the availability of local wage employment. Lastly, all the effects above are contingent upon the extend to which the out-migrant remit food and money to the household in the village.

Alongside reallocation of labour inputs because of out-migration of household members, there may be changes in technology to make better use of the family labour. The new access to information and contacts for employment avenues, can be availed by other prospective migrants through the migrant in the place of destination.

The personal income transfers through remittances made by migrants constitute an important form of reciprocal relationship.

Remittances associated with migration have often being cited as a key benefit for areas of out-migration. Remittances augment savings, investment and technological innovations. Remittances alter the size of distribution of income and aggregate savings behaviour, as well as agricultural productivity and patterns of labour utilisation.

Interview and observations have made it clear that due to remittances made by migrants, the remaining members in the village could able to clear off their debts and maintain their life in a better way. It has created new hope and optimism in their minds and they can visualize the prospects realising their mortgaged plots. It is found from our study that 40% migrants spend in the range of Rs. 4,000 to 4,500 where as 52.6% non-migrants spend below Rs. 3,500/- at an average (Table 4.25 and 4.26). Thus, compared non-migrants, the migrant households spend more expenditure and lead better standard of living.

Further, the findings of the study has already shown that only six migrant households constituting 2.3 per cent of the total one in the debt range of Rs. 4,000/- to above Rs. 6,000/- where as 43 non-migrant house holds where as 43 non-migrant households (16.2%) in the debt position of Rs. 4,000/- to above Rs. 6,000/-. Thus, the position of migrant households are better compared to non-migrant households. (Table 4.27 and 4.28).

Impact of Migration for Area of Origin and Destination

The type of migration flows and the extend of migration, determines the impact of the areas of 'origin' or 'destination'. The effects of migration of destination areas are mere complex, and to examine them requires comparing the socio-economic and demographic situation before and after migration, such as population growth, levels of employment and income, occupational structure, savings and capital formation, structure and composition of industry and levels of Govt. revenue and expenditure. However, besides migration, a wide range of factors determine the change in the situation.

Effects on Wages, Income and Employment

The shift of population to urban areas where incomes are higher creates a growing urban demand for rural output, which changes the rural-urban terms of trade of raising the agricultural prices relative to those of urban goods (assuming Government non-intervention). The hike in agricultural prices by stimulate agricultural production and increase the demand for rural labour. Supply of labour being low, there will be higher rural wages. Permittances of our-migrants are likely to augment rural incomes, and may have an additional effect through technological change.

On the contrary, depending upon the characteristics of migrants, rural-urban migration involves of human capital out of the rural sector, which may adversely affect agricultural productivity and incomes. Thus, it is the ability of the rural households to adopt to the changing scenario and to adopt the new technology for higher productivity that determine their income position.

In the context of urban areas, the exodus of rural migrants adds to the existing problem of unemployment. It aggravates the position of urban unemployment and urban wages. Todaro was of the opinion that migration of rural labour to urban areas is the important reason of growth of the low productive urban informal sectors. However, it is definitely not possible to conclude in advance, that unemployment problem will aggravate because much depends on whether migrants add more to the supply of labour or to the demand for labour or to the demand for labour. To the extent the new arrivers are moderately well educated and highly motivated, total urban production may increases, raising the demand for labour more than the supply. The net effect would be an increase in urban economic growth.

The relationship between migration and labour force participation in rural areas in theoretically indeterminate. Empirical studies have suggested that the participation of migrants in the labour force to a greater extent than natives. This is because of several reasons.

First, migrants are likely to have less support from friends and relatives in their destination areas, and are therefore, under greater pressure to join the urban labour force.

Second, the new migrants have lower levels of aspirations and expectations. Therefore, likely to take up whatever jobs and available. Third, generally migrants are found with higher participation rate.

In toto, the aggregate relationship will depend on the magnitude of migration, the features of migrants etc.

The age-composition of migrants in our study reveals that around 90 percent of migrants of all villages are in the age group of 15 to 45 years, out of which in the range of 26 to 35 age group the highest percentage of 42.2% is represented and 15-25 age-group is 25.9% (Table 4.9). Thus, the productive labourers are transferred to urban area due to migration from rural regions. Our study has revealed that out of eight villages, in six villages there has been 100% flow of migrants to urban areas. Thus, the destination area of the migrants are mostly the urban areas of "out side the state". (Table 4.11). Basing on our study we can conclude that migration leads to the flow of people to urban centres for higher earning, assured source of employment and livelihood. The migrant households experience better living standard and therefore, we can infer that migration results in ameliorating the standard of living of the migrant households. The flow of labour from rural to urban. Centres as a result of migration, has provided adequate employment and income to the households. This has widen the horizon of outlook of the migrant house holds by their exposure to the out-side world. They could experience the hard realities of life and face challenges, problems during the process of their migration.

Migration provided the households to consume certain goods which were previously not available to them. Thus, they could get enough food and maintain higher living standard and thus, efficiency has certainly improved.

The agricultural labourers who virtually possess inadequate land, for cultivation, could make better investment in the form of better seeds, fertilizers, pumpsets and pesticides due to the "remittance" of the migrant work-men.

The consumption of basket of items and clothes reveals that they are generally better off in companion to their days of pre-migration.

Due to migrant workman in a households, usually mere food becomes available for the remaining members. Also availability of agricultural and other works on the basis of wage earning becomes comparatively high.

The migrant workmen after their return could construct better houses and provided better employment to other unemployed labourers who are engaged in house construction activities.

The foregoing analysis clearly demonstrates that migration has its linkages with raising agricultural productivity, in elevating the standard, of living, in freeing them from the clutches of money lenders, in creating further employment, in making available more food items for consumption and finally in ensuring better living standards in the rural economy.

These apart, migration has been responsible for creating awareness for-learning medical care, family planning, sanitation and other aspects. The children of migrant households are provided with better medical care (Table 4.20).

It has been found that some of the migrant households who were mainly unskilled agricultural labourers could develop their skill due to their migration. Some of them could learn in sewing garments, processing food, repairing cycles and scooters, or in the construction of homes.

The flow of labour from rural areas to urban centres and project sites occurs because of certain factors. The data collected regarding the media of migration demonstrates that the main source of migrants entrance to projects sites and work place has been either through unlicensed agents of through friends and relatives. (Table 4.19).

The old migrants furnish data to the new migrants and even take when in their second or third visit to the work place. This mitigates some of the socio-economic tensions of the new migrants. Due to mental arrest, conflict in the family or social harshment sometimes migrant workmen prefer to leave their households and migrate for a change of mind and place. This serves allied purposes of mental relief besides strengthening economic prospects of the migrants the migrants can be aware of the new world outside their native village and cultivate close contact with outsiders. This broadens their outlook and imbibes the idea of Indianness. They could learn the language of others, can came in contact with other cults and culture, social functions and rituals. It helps in respecting the cultures religion and faiths of others and fosters national integration. Interestingly, migration breaks the joint family system, when migrant workman prefers to settle at urban agglomeration and as a result the joint family breaks down. This pressure the family responsibility of separated families. They could settle there households, solve their economic problems individually. The dependents in the altered circumstances attempts to find out opportunities for earning and thus, the unproductive consumers endeavour to discharge labour for something productive. The size of family is generally reduced by adopting innovative methods of family planning. Because the burden of rearing baby is no longer shared by all adult members but shouldered by the separated household. Thus, migration has indirect linkage with controlling population.

Impact of Migration on Technological Change

Labour out-migration may lead to wage hike in rural areas due to migration of potential and productive labour fore causing pressure to the supply of labour. As a result, the labour-saving technological change may be encouraged and greater work participation may take place among the remaining households an the non-migrant households. Thus, change of technology in labour utilisation may be stimulated. Further, the remittances of the migrants may pave the way for such change of technology.

However, the effect of remittances on technological change is difficult to study. Because, it is the nature of the remittances by the members of the house holds in the origin village, that determine the technological changes in rural sector. The size and frequency of remittance, their use for repayment old debts, releasing the mortgaged land holding, purchase of productive inputs like pumpsets or fertilizers determine the progress and promotion of rural technology and ultimately, economic development. The return migrants may bring new ideas to the village for higher output. It is manifested that some of the dadan migrants face intolerable sufferings in the hands of khatadars/contractors, they were not paid their usual wages as promised to them. They suffer untold mental agony, far off from their native place; in the absence of their payments.

Some of migrants who work in far off places could not send remittances regularly. Usually, the members residing in the village substantially depend upon such remittances. When such remittances are totally discontinued, they face untold sufferings. They recourse to borrowing and suffer hardships. They find it much difficult to adjust themselves with the sudden unanticipated change of non-remittance. Ultimately they once again sunk into poverty.

The child migrants and even adults are sometime habituated of visiting cinema, taking intoxicants and wine in the place of destination. They remain far away from their native villages and could enjoy their time in lavish expenditure. This is particularly true in case of Surat workers. Some of them develop the bad habits of smoking, chewing pan and even drinking wine. The cost of such activities and their impact on the society and family can not be easily estimated.

There is lack of human touch and fellow feeling in the family. Migration causes disintegration in the family as some elderly person migrate for better earning and livelihood. The wife and children face some social problems in the hands of moneylenders, Sarpanchs and village gundas. The family disintegration is due to complex factors of high birth rate and large size of the family, degradation of moral and value system, lack of human touch and hostile atmosphere.

Linkage with "Jejaman Pratha"

It is worthwhile to mention that the labour out-migration has serious impact on 'jejman Pratha'. The Varna System which portrays the work and service dimension of various class of people in the society has been gradually declined in the rural scene. The Sardars were originally conferred certain duties and services to be performed in the villages of India. Gradually, the migration of agricultural labourers and people from there class of workers virtually jeopardized the Jejaman System. The centuries old rigidity crumble down giving place to new ideas and new systems. This leads to institutional changes in rural areas. People of other caste began to stand dry cleaning and shops for overcoming such problems of washing and dirty clothes of villagers. The new saloons hair make-up centres, and beauty parlours have replaced the duties of barbers in village area due to their migration.

Effects on Fertility and Demographic Structure of the Population

Rural fertility is effected in several ways by migration. Because migration affects the level and distribution of rural income, which is expected to influence migration. Second, large-scale out-migration of unmarried adult males or female leads to an imbalance in the sex-ratio, making it a stupendous task to settle marriages. Third, heavy emigration of married males in search of employment opportunities can have adverse effects upon family structure, even contributing to family dissolution. In any case, segregation of husbands from wives especially, during life-cycle phase when couples are fertile may lower fertility, at least temporarily. Fourth, the decisions to migrate and to start a family tend to occur at about the same stage in the life cycle. Thus, migration may lead to postponement of marriage. Fifth, in the case of rural-urban migration, increased contact with more modernized sectors may alter the value system of individuals in rural communities leading to lower fertility norms. While all this suggests that migration will contribute to a reduction in fertility, it must be kept in view that to the extent the purpose of the migration is to become married, as is common for women in some areas, then its effect is pro-natalist.

Generally adult young persons migrate to urban areas. As a result, the crude death rates in rural areas decrease. If selective females in their child bearing years migrate to urban areas, leads to increase in the urban proportion of women. As in-migrant women have higher fertility than urban natives in general, this further contributes to an overall increase in urban fertility. The total effects of these changes on the age and sex composition can be a rapid rise in the size of the urban labour force, particularly in the next generation. Thus, in the longer run the exposure of migrants to the urban milieu of lower fertility will generally bring about lower fertility will generally bring about lower fertility norms among in-migration. Thus, there will be an overall decrease in fertility in the country.

Effects on the Availability of Amenities

Rural people have their access to few modern amenities such as schools, hospitals, drinking water, electricity and financial assistance from banks. Out-migration of rural people to urban areas leads to more availability of such facilities by the remaining rural people. The extent of remittance by the migrants also considerably help in purchasing of household durable goods and also for the improvement of housing in rural areas.

The impact of out-migrants in urban areas has also some influence an urban amenities. The influx of migrants into cities increases the demand for infrastructure facilities and social services such schools, hospitals, transport and communications, water, electricity, housing cultural and recreational facilities. Pressures on these service will lead to reduced standard of living on urban areas. Large socio-overhead investments are required to meet the pressing demands of the growing population. The inflow of population to urban areas need to be checked in order to mitigate this heavy pressure on such social services. The influx of migrants is likely to push up rents and land while in destination areas.

In the informal sector of employment and especially in construction projects, the influx of migrants causes decreasing wage as the supply of labour increases. Lower urban wages, increasing labour efficiency, higher supply of labour are the consequent results of such out-migration to urban centres.

Labour-intensive technology may be promoted in urban areas. In a capital scarce and labour plenty economy, employment opportunities can be opened through such large supply of labour in a comparatively lower cost in urban areas. Rural-Urban migration may lead to overall fertility reduction because of lower rate of population growth. The influx of migrants cause deterioration in the quality of urban life. There may be increase of urban poor, if in-migrants, could not be employed. The problem of slum, drainage and environmental hazards may also take place.

It is revealed from the foregoing illustrations, that the overall implications of immigration for national development can not be easily ascertained. It is also not clear whether Government should allow existing flows of migrant or obstruct it for the well-being of the economy at large. To ascertain the exact situation and to formulate guidelines or policy measures, it is imperative to analyse empirically the process of socio-economic change in the country (or major region) and its interrelationship with migrants.

Study of migration on individual household or community level largely depend on the income transfer and remittances by the migrants and also their pattern of use or investments. Thus, through household study or community-level study, through field survey we can examine the impact of migration.

SECTION—B

In the Past, as reported in the Royal Commission on Labour (1931) report, labour migration was more marked off in factories, tea estates, coal fields and other mines who were permanently employed with all benefits.

But in recent decades employment of migrant labour is done through labour contractors, Sardars or Middlemen. They fail to provide permanent employment but exploit the labourers by making less payment to them and taking Commission from the real employer of such labourers.

There are descriptions in the Royal Commission on labour in India (1931) that there were the One lakh migrant labour in Burma employed in textile factories. The indirect employment of unskilled labour is a feature of industry in Burma and especially in Rangoon.

In recent decades labour migration is mostly spectacular in—

i) Construction projects through out the country.

ii) Brick-kilns industries in every part of India.

iii) Sugarcane fields of Gujarat and Maharashtra.

iv) Fish cutting Units in Gujarat, Kerala, Goa and other parts of

India.

The Migrant labourers are under the control of labour contractors and therefore the latter employ them on their own terms and conditions.

As the migrant workmen are employed casually and not permanently, no labour laws were applicable to them. They are deprived of all legal benefits and security of employment by the employers with the collaboration of the cruel contractors.

Though some, Acts like Industrial Disputes Act, 1947, Minimum Wages Act, 1948, Inter-State Migrant Workmen (Regulation of Employment and Condition of Service Act, 1979) have been passed. These acts are never enforced and thereby the poor, illiterate and unorganised labourers suffer hardship in distant lands out-side Orissa.

Maternity Benefit Act, 1961,

Payment of Bonus Act, 1965,

Payment of Gratuity Act, 1972,

Industrial Employment (standing Orders) Act, 1948.

Employment State Insurance Act, 1948.

The recent Act Inter-State Migrant Workmen, 1979 only regulates the condition of services of such labourers who are migrating through labour contractors, But the labour migrating without such contractors are not coming under the purview of such Act. Hence, the displacement allowances were never paid to such labourers and they were subject to numerous exploitations. The Royal Commission on labour in India observed in 1931.

"In India, nearly the whole mass of Industrial labour is illiterate, a state of affairs which is unknown to overestimate the consequences of this disability, which are obvious in wages, in health, in productivity, in organisation and in several other directions. Modern machine Industry depends in peculiar degree in education, and the attempt to built it up with an illiterate body of workers must be difficult and perilous. We would emphasize the fact that precisely because of this, the education of industrial labour should receive special attention."

Economic development, ultimately depends upon the productive skills and the levels of education of the Industrial Labour. Investment in the education of labourers is an investment in the development of human resources urgently required for planned economic development.

If agriculture remains under the grip of the landlords and money lenders, they would naturally have control over the agricultural production and national income, resulting in rampant hoarding and speculation. This prevents the accumulation of capital required for the development of agriculture, which constitutes the vital problem of our economy. The cultural back-wardness of the country can not be removed so long as the peasants forming the majority off the population live in distress and their children are compelled to earn their barest subsistence as wage labour.

The expanding employment opportunities for skilled as well un-skilled labourers are available in a growing city especially in its informal sector like various types of constructions, petty trades, household services and also jobs in public establishments. While there is growing demand for labour in all these new expanding work opportunities, associated with the economic growth of the city, there is increasing unemployment and under employment in different degree in rural areas in India.

The decline in income avenues is largely because of over-crowding on agricultural land as a result of the population explosion, and the absence of commensurate growth of land substituting technology. Particularly hard hit in the process are the sub-subsistence farmers and tribal labourers who have been repeatedly victims of acute distress, and alienate from their land. In areas Bolangir and Kalahandi, the rainfall is low and frequent droughts leads to repeated failure of crops and instability in production. This effects on the one hand the marginal farmers by the damage wrought to their crops beyond their capacity to absorb, and the agricultural labourers on the other, by depriving them of adequate wage income as a sequel to the crop failure. Under these situations, those who live on the brink of acute distress are under compulsion of leaving their villages and seeking their fortune else-where. The decline in employment opportunities in the village is some-times due to the erosion of traditional crafts and professions as a result of competition from the modern sector.

The immediate cause triggering off the migration, leaving behind the age-old hearth and home, may often by some sort of a crisis situation that calls for such desperate action. This causative factor for this is usually heavy indebtedness at disproportional interest rates incurred due to a variety of reasons. The most common one is enforced expenditure on the marriage of a daughter or sister and in some case even of a male member of the family. Once heavy debt is incurred, he sees no way of repaying it except by coming to the city as he feels that the better employment opportunities there will enable him to accomplish the task.

Besides social obligations like marriages, a failure in trade or business transaction, that leaves no hope for a recovery, often leads to indebtedness, and thus once again to migration. Sometimes, it is a case of a family fund or any other cause, leading to costly litigation which brings about involvement in heavy debt and consequential alienation from one's native village.

The study has brought to light that Surat, an old port city, is the second largest city of Gujarat. It is famous for its textile, diamond and Jari industries. The growth of textile industries in Surat is basically due to its black-soil, suitable for cotton cultivation. Including the 'ghost looms' the total number of looms in Surat is more than one Lakh. The textile industries draw the migrant workmen like bees to nectar and provide employment to more than 5 lakhs migrant labourers from Orissa, Andhra Pradesh, Bihar, Rajasthan and Uttar Pradesh.

In thousand textile Mills of Surat about 2.5 Lakhs of Oriya migrants from various districts like Ganjam, Puri, Cuttack are working constituting more than 60 percent of the textile workers. About 1.5 lakhs of Oriya Migrants in textile industries of Surat belong to a single administrative sub-division, Bhajanagar, (Ganjam District of Orissa).

The growing population at Surat city in itself also provides employment to a large number of petty traders and vendors, many of whom are from among the migrant poor.

With the mounting cost of living, poor families find it very difficult to mitigate hunger, if there are too many children.[3]

Child-birth also causes periodical interruptions to the work of women, as also a loss in their health and ability to do hard work. Disease or accidents often impair work and make it necessary to find jobs involving comparatively less strain. The rural poor who migrate with their feet in the city and hearts in the village, can be very largely retained in the rural scene with an alteration of investment in rural devèlopment. There is almost a consensus that the growth of large cities should be deliberately decelerated.

The urban to rural movement of labourers can be possible through large scale rural development works like social forestry, forest-based environmental projects. This will lead to displacement of workers in the slum area.

As a base for various expanding economic activities, the Surat city experiences a constant need for physical expansion. This expansion implies an endless demand for a variety of amenities—the construction and reconstruction of buildings, roads, bridges, water supply, drainage, electricity and so forth. The growth of population and increase in income accompanying the growth of economic activities in the city calls for more and more investments in residences and housing, education and health services, parks and recreation centres, hotels and restaurants, shops and community centres. All these again involve an increase in the tempo of constructions. Then there is the need for maintenance of this ever increasing stock of buildings and structures. All these construction works and their maintenance require a large army of both skilled as well as unskilled labour, and thus act as a major absorber of migrant rural labour for the entire sector of construction industry has so for remained labour intensive and has not been modernised except in a very limited way. This is so because with the abundance of supplies from the villages, labour continues to be cheaper than labour-saving equipment. Thus no significant technological change has percolated into the construction sector to affect its labour absorbing capacity.[1] Another area of employment for the rural poor in the city lies in the service services to the household sector, which is generated by the growing population in middle and high income groups engaged in the occupations of the government, trade, industries, transport and the like in the city. Such employment includes domestic services like cooking, cleaning utensils, washing clothes, sweeping houses and compounds and so forth. In a way the affluence in the city attracts and sustains poverty giving rise to a paradoxical state of co-existence of opulence and penury.[2]

It is found from the study that the friends of non-migrants working in worksite establish the link between the employer and non-migrants, create rapport, liaison and act as touch men for employment of rural unskilled landless agricultural labourers. Also, it is revealed that some unauthorised contractor recruit labourers for various work-sites located at far off distant places and their activities could not be regulated under the provisions of Inter-state migrant workmen (Regulation) Act, 1979. The study has revealed that most of the rural-urban migrants are landless agricultural labourers, the unskilled labourers belonging to the category of scheduled castes and tribes. They have been subjected to varying magnitude of oppression and exploitation by economically and socially better-off sections of the rural population. Various studies and rural labour enquiries have brought to light that the benefits of various statutory and non-statutory schemes have not percolated to the poverty stricken rural population.

The Integrated rural development Scheme and Economic Rehabilitation of the Rural Poor (ERRP) and finally the Jawahar Rojgar Yogjana (JRY) have failed due to their investment loopholes. The selection of beneficiary is not genuine. The need of the hour is to plug the loopholes, strengthening administrative machinery, and development of common property management through participant development. In other words, through education, health services and other welfare and security measures the rural poor should be motivated towards their rights as well as duties. Rural camps, organisations, voluntary societies should be started on massive scale to unite and organise the rural poor. Skills formation, education, consciousness, motivation, involvement of workers in different on going governmental employment oriented programme will go a long way in arresting the trend of out-migration. The labour resources, the human capital can be formed through workers' education and utilisation of their labour can immensely benefit for rural development.

Apart from the economic differentiation emerging from land relations, productivity and the application of science and technology, there are socio-economic gradations associated with the caste system. As a result, the village community in India, has been stagnating for generations. Over a half century since independence there has been a steady migration of rural population to urban areas in a continual search for employment and a better standard of living.

The irony is that the benefits of planned development has not percolated to the disadvantaged rural poor. As a result of which, there has been an enormous growth of marginal and small farmers and landless agricultural labourers. The landless labourer mainly depend on wages as a means livelihood. This is the direct-out-come of the pressure of population on land.

The labour market, whether it be the formal or informal sector of employment, finds itself increasingly pressurized by the consistent inflow of migrants into urban centres.

The urban problem is aggravated due to consistent flow of labour force in the urban areas. Even though the industrialisation, process opens new dimension of employment opportunities for the unskilled labourers migrated from rural areas, but it could not maintain a balance with the additions to the existing labour force. Equally over pressurized is the informal sector in urban areas and could not succeed in engaging the rural migrants in gainful employment. As a result the most crucial problems like basic services and urban employment have emerged prominent in urban centres.

In the light of the above analysis, it is required that the issue of rural-urban migration should not be dealt with in isolation, but in an integrated manner.

Utilisation of physical and human resources results in economic development. Population growth unaccompanied by non-agricultural sector must lead to rural out-migration. Because, when dairying, poultry, forestry or cottage and small-scale industries do not expand so as to absorb the surplus labour, mounting number of people must move to urban centre for employment.

The development of the rural economy alone can solve our colossal problems of unemployment, under-employment , inequality, inflation, inadequate supply of basic necessities to the poor as well as the population explosion, when people can get employment in their own villages, the labour out-migration an the resultant urban slums too could disappear. The strategy for rural development during half a century has not satisfied the aspirations of the people. Millions of rural inhabitants are greatly frustrated.

It is said that if capital intensive technology and large Units go together, they are also said to lead to over-concentration of people in towns for better employment opportunities. This leads to slums social breakdown and crime. It impoverishes the country side, takes away gifted people aggravating the rural condition. It is therefore, suggested that Industry should dispersed to villages or smaller towns. This line of argument goes to Gandhi, and the idealization of the Indian village community in contrast to the corruption and misery of city life.[4]

The planning commission viewed, "Urbanisation is an important aspect of the process of economic and social development as is closely connected with many other problems, such as migration from village to towns, levels of living in rural and urban areas, relative costs of providing economic and social services in town of varying size, provision of housing for different sections of the population, provision of facilities like water supply, sanitation, transport and power, pattern of economic development, location and dispersed of industries, civil administration, fiscal policies, and planning of land use. These aspects are of special importance in urban areas which are developing rapidly."*

In view of the problems associated with urbanisation, steps should be taken to halt the trend of out migration and so that urban problems can be minimized.

Rural-based strategy must inevitably begin with the structural re-organisation of the village economy which is dominated by agriculture and allied activities. This would require a package of measure which includes transfer of land resources from the big (or absentee) landlords to the landlords to the actual tillers of the soil, provision of agricultural intra-structure for fuller exploitation of the land, reduction of social and economic inequalities in the villages and generation of increased employment opportunities for the villages folk, preferably within the periphery of the village itself.

To illustrate the point more elaborately, increased agricultural productivity can raise the level of income of agricultural labourers which in turn, can check the intensity of migration. But it should be noted that the growth of agricultural production is directly connected with the question of land reforms. The agricultural production is not only a problem of technology, such as of good seeds, fertilizers, implements, water etc. These are certainly important but unless the question of feudal land relation and exploitation of the market are resolved, the application of technology must again have to be restricted and will enhance difficulties. The scope of

* Third Five Year Plan, p. 689.

introducing technical developments in agriculture becomes very limited, if land remains concentrated in the hands of a few people (other than the cultivators) and majority of the peasants and agricultural labourers remain landless and destitute, and also if the big landlords have opportunities to exploit them cruelly. Moreover, the supremacy of the big owners prevails, whereas the economic conditions of the poor worsens. It can be well conceived from the history of the so called "Green revolution."

References

1. Majumdar Prasanta & Majumdar Illa. *Rural Migrants in an Urban Setting* (A study of two shanty colonies in the capital city of India) Hindustan Publishing Corporation, Delhi, 1978 P. 126.
2. *Ibid.* p.127
3. *Ibid.* p.134
4. Gandhi, M.K. (1948). *Cent percent Swadeshi, or the Economy of Village Industries*. Third edition, Ahmedabad, Navajivan.

Bibliography

Alam, S.M. *Perspectives on Urbanization and Migration—India and USSR*, Allied Publishers, New Delhi (1987).

Amjad, Rashid (Ed.) *To the Gulf and Back : Studies on the Economic Impact of Asian Labour Migration*, New Delhi (1989)

Banerjee, Biswajit. *Rural to Urban Migration and Urban Labour Market* Himalaya Publishing House (1986)

Barik, B.C. *Rural Migrants is An Urban Setting : A Case Study*. Classical Publishing House, Delhi (1994).

Benaji, D.R. *Slavery in British India*, Bombay (1933)

Behari, Bepin. *Unemployment Technology and Rural Poverty*, Vikas Publishing House Pvt. Ltd. New Delhi (1983).

Breman, Jan. Of peasants, migrants and paupers : Rural labour circulations and capitalist production in west India, Oxford University Press, New Delhi (1985)

Gadgil, D.R. *The Industrial Evolution of India*, Calcutta (1942)

Khan, Nijam. *Pattern of Rural Out-Migration*, B.R. Publishing Corporation, Delhi (1986)

Studies in Human Migration, Rajesh Publishing New Delhi (1983).

Kamble, N.D. *Labour Migration In Indian States*, Ashish Publishing House, New Delhi, (1983)

Mishra R.P. (Ed.). *International Division of Labour and Regional development*, Concept Publishing, New Delhi (1989).

Majumdar, Prasanta S., Majumdar, Illa. *Rural Migrants in An Urban Setting* (A study of two shanty colonies in the capital city of India) Hindustan Publishing Corporation, Delhi (1978)

Mandal, B.R. (Ed.). *Frontiers on Migration Analysis*, Concept Publishing Company, New Delhi (1981).

Premi, Mahendra K. *Urban Out-migration*, A study of its Nature, Cause and Consequences, Sterling Publishers Pvt. Ltd. New Delhi (1980).

Paul, R.R. *Rural-urban Migration in Punjab*, Himalaya Publishing, Bombay.

Raju, B.R.K. *Developmental Migration : A Processual Analysis of Interstate Rural—Rural Migration.* Concept Publishing Co., New Delhi (1980).

Roy, S.N. *Migratory Women Workers: A Study.* Bihar Tribal Welfare Research Institute, Govt. of Bihar, Ranchi.

Sinha, M.M.P. *The Impact of Urbanisation of Land Use in the Rural-Urban fringe: A case study of Patna.* Concept Publishing Company, New Delhi (1980).

Saxena, D.P. *Rural Urban migration in India*, Popular Prakashan, Bombay.

Seshadri, K. *Rural Unrest in India.* Intellectual Publishing House, New Delhi (1983).

Sen, Sukomal. *Working Class of India* (History of Emergence and movement (1830-1970) K.P. Bagehi and Company, Calcutta.

Saha, Panchanan. *Emigration of Indian Labour*, Peoples' Publishing House, New Delhi (1970).

Singh, J.P. *Pattern of Rural Urban Migration in India.* Inter-India Publication, New Delhi (1986).

Sabot, R.H. *Economic Development and Rural Migration Tanzania* (1900-1971), Clarendon Press, Oxford, (1979).

Sinha, V.N.P. & Ataullah, Mohammad. *Migration : An Inter-disciplinary Approach.* Rajesh Publication, New Delhi (1987).

Tripathy, S.N. *Bonded Labour in India*, Discovery Publishing House, New Delhi, (1989).

------ *Exploitation of Child labour in Tribal India.* Daya Publishing House, New Delhi (1991)

------ *Informal Women Labour in India*, Discovery Publishing House, New Delhi (1991).

------ *Agricultural Labour in India*, Discovery Publishing House, New Delhi (1996).

------ *Migrant Child labour in India.* Mohit Publication, New Delhi (1997).

Thorner Alice & Daniel. *Land and Labour in India*, Asia Publishing House, Bombay, (1962).

Weiner, Myron. *Sons of the Soil: Migration and Ethnic Conflict in India*, Oxford University Press, Delhi (1978).

Index